I'D RATHER *Eat* CHOCOLATE

I'D RATHER

Eat

CHOCOLATE

....

Learning to Love
My Low Libido

....

JOAN SEWELL

BROADWAY BOOKS
NEW YORK

BROADWAY

PUBLISHED BY BROADWAY BOOKS

Published in the United States by Broadway Books, an imprint of
The Doubleday Broadway Publishing Group, a division of
Random House, Inc., New York.
www.broadwaybooks.com

BROADWAY BOOKS and its logo, a letter B bisected on the diagonal,
are trademarks of Random House, Inc.

The events described in this memoir are factually accurate, although the
names of several individuals have been changed to protect their privacy, and
the order of events has been changed in places to organize the flow of ideas.

Grateful acknowledgment is made to quote from the following:

From *Hot Monogamy* by Patricia Love and Jo Robinson, copyright © 1994 by
Patricia Love and Jo Robinson. Used by permission of Dutton Signet,
a division of Penguin Group (USA) Inc.

From *Redbook's Married Lust* by Pamela Lister and Redbook Magazine.
Excerpted with permission from *Redbook's Married Lust* by Pamela Lister and
Redbook Magazine, copyright © 2001 by Hearst Communications, Inc.

Book design by Jennifer Ann Daddio

Library of Congress Cataloging-in-Publication Data

Sewell, Joan.
I'd rather eat chocolate : learning to love my low libido /
Joan Sewell. — 1st ed.
p. cm.
1. Sexual desire disorders—Popular works.   2. Sex therapy—Popular works.
3. Women—Sexual behavior.   I. Title.

RC560.S46.S493 2007
616.85'83—dc22
2006022399

ISBN: 978-0-7679-2267-8

PRINTED IN THE UNITED STATES OF AMERICA

1   3   5   7   9   10   8   6   4   2

First Edition

To my husband

Kip

for his love, honesty, and

unflagging encouragement in the writing of this book

Contents

I'D RATHER *Eat* CHOCOLATE

One

HOW MUCH SEX
DID YOU SAY?

f I had a choice between reading a good book and having sex, the book wins. I notice I put in the adjective "good"—and that leaves me wondering if I'm not trying to put a better face on things. I still want people to read this and think, *Well, of course. If it's a good book.* But my boyfriend—the man I would eventually marry— would take even bad sex over a good book.

CURIOSITY KILLS THE CAT

Then I asked the question that really started the dominoes falling: I finally got the nerve to ask my boyfriend if he could have as much sex as he wanted, how much would that be? The fact is we hadn't directly addressed our sex lives, even though we were way along into the relationship. We'd surely had our problems. But at this particular moment, my question was only half serious: casual curiosity after reading an article on men and sex in a glamour magazine.

"As much sex as I wanted?" Kip sat down on the edge of the bed and slowly took off his shoes. I knew what he was thinking.

"Yeah. As much as you wanted," I repeated.

Kip delayed answering by adopting a puzzled look of concentration as if the question would *never* have occurred to him before my asking it. "Oh, I don't know . . . maybe about five or six times a week."

My eyebrows shot up into outer space. "Wow. Really?"

"Yeah, I'd probably want one day off."

I looked intently at him. Was he joking? I decided he wasn't. "That wouldn't tire you out? Every day?"

"No. It doesn't have to be a big production or anything."

"Right."

"Four or five days can be just . . . you know . . . plain . . ."

"Meat-and-potatoes sex."

"Yeah." He knew what that meant from our discussions about *Mars and Venus*. "And a couple of times a week I'd like gourmet sex." *Mars and Venus* again, code for extra-fancy sex.

"Gourmet sex twice a week? Wow." "Wow" was becoming my favorite fill-in exclamation. It shows surprise without necessarily designating a judgment.

"Well, really, I'd be happy with it once a week." He was making an effort to make his fantasy sex life more realistic. It wasn't working for me.

"Well, okay, um . . . Wow." *Yikes!*

Kip walked into the kitchen and got a Coke out of the fridge. I stood in the middle of the living room in wonder at how far apart we were. My arms were crossed over my chest as I stared down at the carpet. I concentrated on taking even breaths.

"Of course I don't *expect* that," Kip called out from the kitchen. "That's just my fantasy. No woman is going to want sex every day."

"How do you know? Maybe there are women who do want sex almost every day. Maybe you just didn't look hard enough."

He walked back into the living room with the tiniest of smirks on his face. "Uh-huh. How many women are picking up guys for sex?"

"Some."

"Not a lot." Kip screwed off the bottle cap and took a couple of swallows.

"Well, even if it is rare to find a woman who wants that much sex, shouldn't you try anyway? Why settle?" I was feeling pettish by now.

"Because she doesn't *exist*."

Who was he trying to reassure, him or me? Of course she existed, just in smaller numbers. But didn't he owe it to himself to try to find someone sexually compatible before settling for less? I didn't want him to be deprived and unhappy, I didn't want to be the one who held him back, I didn't want to be the one he settled for. More than that, I was tired of always feeling apologetic for my drive.

Kip sat down at his swivel chair and turned toward his desk. His way of saying, Enough, I'm not going to deal with this anymore. But I couldn't let it lie.

TEARS AND WHISPERS

Clicking by the channels, I caught Oprah in midspeech saying that millions of women don't want sex. She said low female libido is a problem that is, in her words, "big, big, big, big, big." Whoa. I lunged for a blank videotape and tore open the packaging with my teeth. I jammed it into the VCR and sat down. "Thank you, *thank you,* talk-show gods." With immense relief I listened to how millions of women were silently suffering in shame. Though there are books dealing with loss of desire in women that I read in private desperation, the literature didn't come close to the impact of seeing women on television in tears and listening to their words of despair over their low sex drives. Many of the women Oprah had on her show were young women in young marriages. Oprah was telling her audience, speaking to the camera, that you're not alone, millions of women have this hidden shame. I can only say I felt a mixture of exhilaration and gratitude while I watched. Somebody was talking about it, real people, and not just the sexperts. Women were talking about the pain, fear, insecurity, guilt, and shame of having low sexual desire. Yes. This *is* big.

> TERRI: We have sex about every four to five months. This is a lot less than what my husband would like. I don't enjoy sex. I dread it. My husband's thought about divorce because of it. It would be totally fine if I never had sex again.
>
> SHANNA: We are in our first year of marriage and we get along fine except for one thing. I never want to have sex with him. I'm never in the mood. I'm afraid that he's going to get tired of a sexless marriage and leave.
>
> SAMANTHA: In our five years of marriage we have fought over and over about sex and my lack of desire. My husband has turned away from me. It makes me a nervous wreck.

BETTY: My marriage would be practically sexless if it were up to me. I've become totally uninterested, almost repulsed.

MICHELLE: Before we were married, we would have sex probably three or four times a week. Ever since we've been married, our sex life is more "let's get it over with." It's more a dread type thing. Some days, I do think it's dirty and nasty.

Women are using words like "dread" and "repulsion" and referring to sex as a personal invasion. Oprah notes seeing members of the audience in tears. Tears and dread and invasion. I think, "My God, are we just lying there taking it and faking it?" Judging by the above quotes, the answer is apparently yes.

HOT, HOT, HOT

But there were other shows telling me the opposite is true. On their cable television program, *Berman & Berman: For Women Only,* sister sexperts Laura and Jennifer Berman sent out one of their people to interview women on the street, and the word is women want a lot more sex:

FEMALE INTERVIEWER: How often do you have sex?

WOMAN #1: As often as possible.

WOMAN #2: Three to four times a week.

WOMAN #3: I'm single, so I take sex when it is possible.

INTERVIEWER: How often is that?

WOMAN #3: One or two a month.

INTERVIEWER: How often do you have sex with your
    partner?
WOMAN #4: When I have a partner. Three or four times a
    day.
INTERVIEWER: A day?
WOMAN #4: Well yeah, with the right partner.
DR. LAURA BERMAN: That's the key.
DR. JENNIFER BERMAN: With the *right* partner.
LAURA B: With the right partner, but you can see there's a
    range.

I can't imagine having sex three or four times a day. I just can't.
Even the Bermans' effort to show what constitutes a wide range of
frequency still leaves me feeling bruised. I can't even make it to
the low end. So, I'm still the odd girl out. But just when I was feeling down about not wanting sex at least every other day, Jennifer
Berman took it down a notch for married folks:

JENNIFER B: But once you're in, you know, married,
    routine life, I think about two to three times a week is
    pretty normal.
LAURA B: For *you*. Yeah. I mean it really is personally
    defined. But I want to hear what our audience thinks.
ROXANNE: And first of all let me tell you my disclaimer is
    I've been married a long time. Almost thirteen years.
    And we have sex about once a week . . .
LAURA B: . . . Yeah. What else. Who else? Does anyone
    else have another answer? What about right here?
    What's your name?
BIANCA: Hi. My name is Bianca. And I'm in a great

relationship. And for me, three to four times a week is
great. But I would personally settle for seven.

LAURA B: Seven times?

JENNIFER B: Seven times a week. Every day.

LAURA B: And you know that's nice because we're hearing
that on tape and in the audience. The myth is that
women aren't really game or wanting to have sex as
much. And these women are saying, "Hey, anytime I
can get it."

God, I feel so inadequate.

The one woman on this show who said she had sex only once a
week was apologetic about it, asking for understanding . . . you see,
we've been married for thirteen years. Why was she apologizing? In
the face of all these randy women, she felt abnormal. It's how I feel
even when watching from the safe distance of my living room. The
Bermans don't make me feel better about myself. The more they
educate me, the more I'm cast as the outsider, the dysfunctional
wife, the inhibited, repressed, hormonally deficient problem child.
Even though the Bermans are careful to say what's considered normal should be taken on an individual basis, they still are framing a
range. Jennifer pulled the two-to-three-times-a-week statistic out
of the air, while the rest of the show quoted women who wanted it
every day or at any opportunity, whichever comes first. Then, with a
touch of triumph, the Bermans ended their program saying that
from what women were telling them, it's a myth that we don't want
sex as much as men—we're trying to get it as much as we can.

So which is it? Are women more like the tearful bunch seen on
Oprah or like the sexual enthusiasts on *Berman & Berman*?

Two

FREQUENCY

efore our marriage, Kip and I had sex from three to four times a month according to my Faux Spontaneity Plan. The plan was really quite simple: have sex once a week for three weeks and you get one week off for good behavior. I might pleasantly surprise my man with a fourth week in a row some months, alternating with three-week months. That was only to show I was not actually planning a week off. But I did plan it. Three times a month, and the fourth time was the wild card, or in baseball terms, the change-up. Why choose once a week? I suppose it seemed like that was the general marker of time that's permissible to not have sex before my boyfriend started making scratches on the bedroom wall marking the days.

I wanted to know exactly where I stood in comparison to the

national average. But I found that self-help books and sexperts are amazingly coy about sexual frequency. The experts try to wave away the appearance of having any interest in numbers, but they do show their biases.

HOW MUCH IS NORMAL?

One book with the irresistible title *Not Tonight Dear* claims, "Any man or woman is bound to prefer good sex twice a week to bad sex every night." It sounds to me like twice a week is being offered as the *low* end of the scale (but it still can be okay if the sex is good). There are several times when the authors casually refer to having sex a "couple of times a week" as if it were an off-the-top-of-their-head example, even as it serves to establish that number as the norm. Any way you looked at it, I was clearly out of the running for what constitutes normal sexual relations.

But I read an article in *Newsweek* that said statistics on sex might be unreliable given the current climate associating sex with solid relationships, good mental health, and emotional maturity:

> *Any efforts to quantify our love lives must be taken with a shaker of salt. The problem, not surprisingly, is that people aren't very candid about how often they have sex. Who wants to sound like a loser when he's trying to make a contribution to social science? When pressed, nearly everyone defaults to a respectable "once or twice a week," a benchmark that probably seeped into our collective consciousness with the 1953 Kinsey Report, a study that's considered flawed because of its unrepresentative, volunteer sample.*

Well, flawed though it may be, it hasn't stopped the twice-a-week average from being adopted as a healthy minimum in a lot that I read and hear on talk shows. But thinking about my own marriage, I wondered if the twice-a-week average might also be in part the product of a compromise between the frequency of sex that men would love to have and the frequency women are willing to live with.

LETTING IT SLIDE

Patricia Love's book *Hot Monogamy* deals with couples who have major sex-drive differences. For example, Love talks about one of her low-desire clients, Pam, who wants sex only three to four times a month. Love categorizes Pam as "rarely" wanting sex. I'm insulted. In my playbook, I'd call three or four times a month about right.

For some men, once-a-week sex is not good enough or kinky enough to keep them smiling through the next six days. And they're going to let their wives or girlfriends know it in one way or another. For other men, once a week is barely enough for their tastes, but they may dislike pushing for more because of the endless arguments the wife or girlfriend may bring to bear on why she finds sex during the week so difficult. Or, like Kip, a man may feel ashamed of wanting more sex with his wife when she clearly doesn't want much sex with him.

Sure, motivating yourself to have sex twice a week will keep you in that magical statistical realm and out of the therapist's chair. Still, even once a week, and we all kind of knowingly laugh—nothing that a little time management, romance, and a trip to Victoria's Secret won't fix. Once a week usually means having Saturday-night no-excuses-left sex. Some of us down that whiskey or hide in the bathroom having a precourage cigarette or joint before making our triumphant entrance into the bedroom, all sexy smiles and lingerie. Less than once a week and you're looking pretty bad. You have a desire disorder. Boy! Now what do I do, Doc? Your relationship with your man will be gone over with a fine-tooth comb; your past will be examined for any signs of negativity about sex from parents, friends, teachers, priests, rabbis, or whoever. Oh, I know, I went through it.

The Faux Spontaneity Plan got us through early courtship, but then our frequency dropped from sex three or four times a month for about a year to sex twice a month. That's when our real troubles began.

Three

I'M NOT IN THE MOOD

One night Kip and I were lying in bed. He started kissing my neck and rubbing my thigh. I scooched away from him, but not wanting to seem rude, I gave him the excuse that it tickled. Then he reached over to tickle my ribs, thinking that I was being playful. I angrily told him, "Hey, cut it out!"

Kip looked stunned. "What? You were laughing!"

"I was laughing because it tickles. Just a knee-jerk response. Look, I'm real tired, and if you get me all stimulated and everything, I won't be able to get to sleep. You know I need my sleep or I go crazy. I've got lots of stuff to do at work tomorrow and I've got to be able to concentrate, okay?"

"Jeez, all right, all right. Never mind. I *get* it."

I continued to dodge sex with Kip by indicating in very unsubtle ways just how stressed I was. First I would tell him how bad a day I was having; now I started saying how bad a week I was having, hoping to knock out more potential days of sex with one stone. "Kip, let me just get through this week with my sanity."

But I knew he was doing everything he could, hoping to ease my day. He'd surprise me by ordering Chinese, or taking me out to our favorite restaurant, or getting me roses. He'd take me out for strolls around Coventry Village, a Bohemian 'burb just outside my home town of Cleveland. He'd clean the kitchen or run out and get me a scoop of my favorite ice cream when I was blue. Every morning I'd wake up to a cup of coffee made exactly the way I liked it. After doing all these things time and again, week after week and month after month, and listening to me vent about my arduous life over and over, Kip wasn't buying it anymore. I never had a good day, I never had a good week. I knew he thought the stress thing was more than a little bull.

One night, when I rebuffed him again as he nestled next to me, Kip sat up in bed, leaned against the headboard, and crossed his hands behind his head.

"Joan, just tell me, do you not like sex? Just tell me without all this hemming and hawing. Because if you don't, I can accept that. What I can't accept is this"—he waved his arms trying to look for the right word—"this charade. Because you're making me miserable and yourself miserable, too. I need to know. I don't want to play around with this anymore."

I felt totally cornered. I swallowed hard. How much should I admit to? Did I even know the whole story myself? I had to say something.

"I really don't know myself," I said. Kip looked at me doubtfully. I continued: "I guess I don't want to think too closely about it." He sighed. I was dancing again.

"Just be straight with me. Do you or do you not like sex? You should know the answer to that."

I stayed quiet for such a long time that Kip got up off the bed and said, "I think I got my answer."

"Truthfully? Most of the time, I just don't think about it. And"—I sighed because this was going to be a tough one for him to swallow—"even if I do have a good time or orgasm—it's nice, but I don't know if it's always worth the effort to me. Sometimes, but . . ." Not even the Holy Grail of orgasm was enough to muscle up my libido. "What I mean, I guess, is that I don't have a frequent urge for sex. I don't."

"Yeah, I know. You hardly have any urge. Not from what I can tell, unless you have some secret I don't know about."

I brought my knees up to my chin and said quietly, "No. No, I don't."

Kip walked out of the bedroom and then walked back in. He said gently, "Well, this is not the kind of relationship I had in mind."

"We fooled each other, didn't we? You said that yourself."

He sat back down on the bed and rubbed my back. "I know, but I didn't think it would become this out of balance. You're not interested in sex with me?"

"Kip, it isn't about you, it's about me." I knew that sounded trite.

He turned to look at me. "What can we do?"

"Let's just try again, okay. Let's wipe the slate clean and try again. No baggage. No bullshit."

And try we did. For almost two months. We were having sex at least twice a week. I got a clue from one of my pals, Diane, and decided to work a short session in once or twice a week, and then, once in a while, a longer sex session on the weekends. This lasted all of six weeks. By the end of the second month, I was back to my old ways. Kip, darn him, somehow took notice. No sneaking lack of sex by him.

"It's not working out again," Kip told me. "I don't want to end our relationship. I love you, and I want to be with you. But I need to know what to expect if this relationship is going to work. Just tell me if you want to go platonic, or what?"

"I know. I understand," I said miserably. "Maybe we should go to a couples' counselor or something. I want to work this out and apparently, I don't know how to."

He didn't like the idea of going to a therapist, but I convinced him. I needed to know what was going on.

ON THE COUCH

e sat nervously in the waiting room not speaking to each other. I thought it was because we weren't sure if one of us might say something that would put the other in a bad light. Man, I just knew I was the one who was going to get hammered. I anxiously rubbed my sweaty palms up and down my pants.

A tall, thirty-something woman with long, blond hair came out of the office. She wore a cream-colored, closely fitted, and obviously well-tailored blazer. Peeking through the lapels of her blazer was the lacy top of a lavender camisole. I wondered if she'd notice the lint on my black pants. In the light of my bathroom they seemed fine. Out in the daylight it looked like I had rolled around and around on an old carpet.

"Kip and Joan? Hi, I'm Julie. Please come in," she said.

IN OUR OWN WORDS

Julie, a couples' counselor, was to be our sex therapist. We followed her into her office. A few feet from the wall there was a long couch and parked uncomfortably near to it was a lone chair, a wingback, that I supposed was hers. Unsure of how close together or far apart we should sit (what might it psychologically indicate?), we ended up leaving a cushion between us.

"Tell me why you're here," said Julie.

She knew why we were there, but it's the therapist's trick to make us put it into our own words.

Kip looked over at me, hesitating about who should go first. The pause had made me uncomfortable enough that I couldn't out-wait it. "It's because we're not in sync . . . sexually," I said.

"All right, where do you want to start?" she asked, looking from me to Kip.

Well, where I wanted to start was with her skirt. After we had said our hellos and sat on the couch, she had taken her seat in the chair and crossed her legs. Her skirt, which was on the short side but perfectly respectable when she stood, had ridden up to the up-per part of her thighs. And, my God, were those four-inch heels? Who was this woman, Ann Coulter?

"I don't think Joan is interested in sex," Kip was saying, more bluntly than I had anticipated.

"Is that right, Joan?" she asked.

"Well . . ." Where do I go from here? He was right. That about summed it up. Let's say g'day and I'll take my sexless little behind home.

"Do you have *any* interest in sex?"

"Uh, yeah," I said in a helium squeak. "But not much. For all intents and purposes, it amounts to . . . not much."

Julie leaned forward and leveled her eyes at me. She said in a confidential tone, "Are you comfortable talking about it in front your boyfriend?"

"Yeah, sure." No.

Then I wondered if Kip was getting turned on by her legs. He must have been really working to avoid staring at them. Even *I* was working hard to avoid staring at them.

"Well, let me tell you my usual protocol. We'll have separate sessions. One session I'll talk to you, Joan. Another day I'll talk to Kip. Eventually, I'll talk to both of you. The sessions will be twice a week until we get to the point where both of you are attending the same session. Does that sound all right to you?"

"I guess so," I replied. Not wanting to exclude Kip, I looked at him and asked, "What do you think, honey?" I added the "honey" in a sunny voice to show how all lovey-dovey we still were.

"Yes," he said, "we can do that."

"But today," Julie continued, "I'll be taking a little background of your relationship. How long has this problem been going on?"

"Almost since the beginning," said Kip.

"Joan, do you agree?"

I hesitated. I was trying to think of some time when Kip and I were in the Garden of Eden and having sex and eating caramel apples and delighting in each other's body as we jumped like Lords a' Leaping through flora and fauna. But alas, the answer was . . . Yes . . . true . . . yes.

GOING SOLO

It was my idea to try a therapist, so I was determined to give it a go. Even so, I wasn't looking forward to my first solo session with Julie. I already thought she'd be against me. Plus, I knew we wouldn't be on the same wavelength. She had the Vaseline smile and hard edge usually associated with ex–beauty queens who drove beyond peach festivals to land the big fish, the state finals. I, on the other hand, distrust people who smile gamely at me, especially when I know they're thinking I couldn't win a Miss Tuber contest if I tried. Maybe I'm just being paranoid. I tried smiling back.

"All right, why don't we begin today with what you find positive in your sexual relationship with Kip. I find looking at the positives first gives us a nice foundation to start from." She gave me a face that said she either wanted my blessing or my congratulations.

"Sounds good," I said simply.

"Have you had any good sexual experiences with your boyfriend?"

"Yes."

"That's good!" she said too brightly. "And what do you think made those experiences good?"

"I don't know." I shrugged. I didn't know. I couldn't think of anything specific.

She tried to help me by asking a more concrete question: "Were there some things that Kip did or didn't do at those times that made you enjoy sex more?"

I thought. "Not that I can think of." I paused. "I don't think it has anything to do with his performance, if that's what you're asking. So, that's why it's hard for me to answer that question. That's what you're talking about, right?"

"Well, yes. It could be physical, but it also could be romantic, or how he made you feel emotionally."

"Well, like I said, he's fine in the physical department. He's willing to do anything I want—you know, if I need to be stimulated in a certain way. And I can orgasm . . . but it just doesn't translate into me wanting more sex."

"We'll come back to that," Julie said. "But let's move on to the emotional side of sex for you."

I told her that Kip was emotionally good for me. He really was. He did everything you could think of to make me feel at ease. And he was very romantic. Even in everyday stuff. He was a cuddler and a snuggler. I got plenty of affection from him.

"All right, let's take some time to explore your attitude toward sex. Let's see if we can delve a bit into your past to see if there are any old influences that are still affecting you.

"Let's start here: Who taught you about sex? Your parents?"

"No, they didn't say anything about sex," I said. "My mother only told me about periods."

"Where *did* you learn about sex?"

"Some sort of biology class in the seventh grade."

"So your introduction to sex was clinical," said Julie. "You didn't have a role model to tell you about the emotional side." She sounded like she was fitting together the pieces of an already familiar puzzle.

I acquiesced to the answer I knew she wanted to hear: "I guess not."

"Perhaps not hearing about sex from your parents led you to think sex was bad."

"I don't think so." Julie gave me the slightest squint. That puzzle piece didn't fit. *They didn't tell me about love, either, and that didn't make me think love was bad.*

"Well, it could affect how you view sex now," she said with great gravity. Smash that puzzle piece into place.

"Really?" I put a hint of wide-eyed facetiousness in my tone . . . or is it sarcasm? I wondered if she'd detect it. I wondered if I'd ever remember the difference between facetiousness and sarcasm.

"Your parents were your primary relationship," Julie stated. "They are the model that children base their views on relationships between men and women."

"Uh-huh." Blah, blah, blah.

"Did your parents freely show each other affection?"

"Not really."

"What was your relationship with your father?" How cliché.

"The usual cliché stuff. He worked a lot, was distant, mowed the lawn on the weekends. Not much to talk about. Look, I don't think this will get us anywhere."

"Okay, I'm just wondering what message was sent if your parents didn't show affection in front of you and stayed silent about sex. It might have signaled to you that sex was somehow bad or dirty because physical affection was not something that should be displayed or even talked about."

I knitted my brow to appear as if I was putting great thought into my answer. I folded my hands together on my lap and said, "No, really, I don't think so." And I didn't. After watching TV sexperts and reading self-help books, you get acquainted with the usual questions—and I already knew the answers.

"Children absorb even unspoken messages from their parents," she persisted.

"True, but . . ." I think I already understood that and had delved as far into it as I could go. "I still don't think it's got anything to do with my parents. If anything, I learned sex was dirty mostly from boys and even a few girls.

"Maybe it's a, uh, a . . ."—I searched for some word other than the gratingly overused self-esteem—"a confidence issue." Then I began confessing: "And when I was in grade school, and part of junior high, I was painfully shy back then. Gawky. My clothes were wrong. My hair was wrong. I had glasses. Eventually, when my mother stopped insisting I wear geek clothes, I bought contacts and my breasts came in big-time. But I never felt at ease in my own body."

This news very much pleased Julie. It was all coming together: unaffectionate parents, distant father, dirty-mouthed boys, and an ugly-duckling phase that probably scarred my self-esteem.

"So many girls go through what you have, Joan. And when they grow into womanhood, they still drag that old picture of themselves with them."

"Uh-huh," I said, sitting up a little.

"Feeling unattractive to the opposite sex *really* does impact how sexy a woman feels." She seemed to put great stress on the word "really" as if she thought I was going to dismiss her once again. But I didn't because suddenly the humiliation felt by that gawky, adolescent girl had become vivid once again and I wanted validation for how much it had hurt.

"That may be why you find it hard to be sexually responsive. A woman can't feel sexual if she feels ugly. You may feel you don't deserve sex. That sex is for beautiful women and that if you fall short of that . . ."

"—that I don't deserve sex, right."

All this was being put together as if in a nexus that would foretell my inability to enjoy sex on a regular basis. But I still had my doubts. Julie seemed too quick to fit me into what I suspected was a rather convenient model.

DAMNED IF YOU DO

Kip picked me up from the therapist and asked me on the drive back home how it went. "I don't know," I said. "It was okay, I guess. I don't think the stuff she asked was very relevant." Then I added, "*And* I think she's kind of snotty."

Kip said, "You do? I don't know, I liked her. To me she seems really nice and I think she knows what she's doing."

"What? How do you know that? You haven't even had a solo session with her yet. How do you know if she's nice and knows what she's doing? We only met with her the first time for what— less than a half hour?"

"Hey, that's just my impression, okay?"

"What, based on her looks?"

"You're just nuts," he said as he parked the car in the lot of our apartment building.

I apologized. I wasn't giving Julie a chance. I explained how having a sexy sex therapist could be a little threatening, considering our situation. He nodded and thanked me for my apology and went into the bedroom to watch the video he'd rented. It was probably some flick with Demi Moore as an aggressive can't-wait-to-rip-your-clothes-off kind of woman. Kip knows I hate Demi Moore. I think that's part of the reason he likes her so much.

I was still troubled by Julie's conclusions and that made me restless. But I couldn't exactly say why I was still so skeptical. I just felt like I was being inserted into a formula. Then I came up with an idea to test her theories. I walked into the bedroom.

"You're not watching Demi Moore, are you?"

"Huh? Demi Moore? What are you talking about?"

"Never mind. Could you just put that on pause for a minute. I need to ask you some questions."

Kip adjusted the bolster in back of him. He looked straight ahead and asked, "What's this about?"

"It's going to sound silly. But I want to know if the same stuff that Julie says affects me sexually has the same effect on you."

Kip tilted his head with mild curiosity. "Okay, shoot."

I asked Kip about his past. I knew a good part of it, but now I wanted to look at it through a therapist's eyes. Kip's father was a border patrolman and that took him away from his family for weeks at a time. While my own father may have been distant, Kip's father was absent for long stretches of his boyhood. I asked Kip when his father had told him about the birds and the bees. But Kip said that it was his mother who explained the mechanical aspects to him.

"Your mom? How'd that go?" I asked.

"I was bored. I already knew about most of it."

"Where from?"

"I knew some of the basics from older kids who knew more than me. Then I got a few more of the details from an after-school special on TV. It had a bunch of teenagers learning about sex from an adult, with animated segments illustrating the finer points of sperm-and-egg uniting—cartoon faces on the sperm flying through tunnels, that sort of thing." Kip pulled up a knee and started to show interest in his own reflections. "Then there were the *Playboy* magazines—I told you that story already—that one of the older kids in my neighborhood kept in his makeshift 'clubhouse.' "

I went right down the line asking Kip some of the questions that Julie had asked me: Kip's family was also not a demonstrative bunch. And they weren't the type of people who talked about feelings. But that's pretty typical of a lot of rural folks who came from a hardscrabble life in the plains.

"Would you say you had a pretty high libido?"

"Me? Oh, yeah—of course. I don't think it was any higher than other guys, but yes, definitely."

But he did fear for his soul. During high school, Kip had become a born-again Christian. He feared his libido was a sign that he would be damned and so he prayed to be released from his preoccupation with sex. But even prayer and faith could not overcome his feelings of lust.

Kip rolled over onto his stomach and leaned on his elbows. "I mean, I tried. I really, really tried. When I kept failing, I felt worthless. I was disgraced in the eyes of God."

I felt bad for him.

"It's okay," he said. "By the time I hit the end of my first year of college, I was on my way out of being born-again. So I wasn't worried about lusting anymore."

Then, as I knew, there was the acne. Smooth and handsome now, Kip had had a bad case of acne that followed him from junior high to his sophomore year in high school. It made him feel very unattractive and self-conscious, unable to approach a girl—for a conversation, let alone a date, even though he had a major crush—who failed to notice him.

"So throughout feeling like an acne-riddled high schooler, a shy, poverty-stricken college student who thought he was prerejected by women—you still had a pretty big sex drive."

"Right, that was a constant—even a thorn in my side."

Well, I thought, Kip's drive was not affected by fear of damnation, an absent father, feeling ugly, fear of rejection, and one heart-wrenching case of unrequited love. If that was the case, then why did Julie think that anything and everything that crossed *my* path was responsible for my lax libido? Even if people vary on an individual basis, I couldn't figure out why so many things in my past would supposedly cripple my libido while many of the same things that Kip experienced had had no effect at all on his robust sex drive. Something wasn't ringing true about Julie's diagnosis.

Five

....

UNSAFE SEX

....

I was back on the long sofa looking at the crossed legs of Ms. Thing. It reminded me of the scene in *The Cat in the Hat* when all you saw of the mother was a pair of legs.

I was by now far more skeptical of Julie than before. Though I wanted to challenge her on what I thought was her dubious reasoning, I chickened out at the last minute. Part of why I did that was that I still had no clue why I had a low libido. Second, I didn't want Kip to think I was trying to demolish her for my own jealous little reasons.

Julie had recapped our last visit: my introduction to sex was basically a negative experience and that prevented me from seeing it as a physical expression of love and trust. She added, "A lot of girls develop a negative view of sex when they are first introduced to it. It can forever change how they view men. Then, as women, they may no longer feel safe around any man, even their own significant others."

"*Really?*" I replied, as if struck by her incisiveness. I had heard of this emotional safety gambit not a few times on talk shows and in self-help books.

She leaned toward me. "Surprising, isn't it?"

"It *certainly* is," I said, as if awestruck. "But, um, I really do feel safe with my boyfriend."

"*Sexually* safe?"

"I'm sorry, what do you mean?"

"When I ask how safe you feel sexually around your boyfriend, I mean how sexually confident do you feel? How open do you feel? Are you able to share your fantasies? Most of all, does the thought of making love to your boyfriend give you a feeling of warmth, intimacy, *safety*?"

That was a tough question. If I took sexual safety in Julie's sense, then really, I didn't feel safe at all. I didn't feel confident sexually, even with my own boyfriend. I even felt scared, like a little kid asked to walk up to the chalkboard in front of the class and do a math problem. I didn't feel a warm, fuzzy feeling when it was time to "make love." I felt . . . incompetent.

"That's what I mean by safety," Julie had gone on to say. "When you feel safe with your partner, it means you can be vulnerable with him. It means he is that warm place you come to for nurturing, for comfort, for *safety*."

SECOND THOUGHTS

After my session, I found Kip in the waiting room for Julie's office. He had come to pick me up. "Wow," I said when we got to the parking lot. It started to rain so we jogged to the car. Kip unlocked my door and I scooted in and unlocked his side. "Put on the heat, put on the heat!" I said. I was wet but happy. I rubbed the raindrops off my arms. *I'm getting to the bottom of it, I'm getting to the bottom of it,* I sang in my head. No wonder! I never knew how to relate to men! I snapped on my seat belt and said to Kip, "You know, I didn't like her at first, but I think she's getting to the bottom of it."

"Well?" Kip asked.

"Okay, it sounds weird, but Julie thinks that maybe I don't feel safe enough with you."

"Uh-huh," Kip grunted with wariness.

"Yeah, I know, I know. But just listen, it's about a *feeling* of safety." I rushed on before he could take it the wrong way. "I wouldn't feel safe with *any* man because I don't know how to fully trust. And if I can't do that, I can't open up. Instead I have my guard up. See, it's mostly me—not you."

"I know you're not the most trusting person in the world, but what is she saying—that you don't trust me enough to have sex? How long do you have to know me? We've been together for *over two years*. I don't get it."

He was insulted. But who wouldn't be? I told him it had nothing to do with how long we'd been together because this was a core thing I'd had for a long time. And since I was unaware of it, it kept quietly influencing how I perceived sex, love, and men. "Julie said it's not about lust or hormones, it's about feeling secure enough to open up to a man. She said there are lots of women like me who have the exact same problem."

"Yeah, that's something all right," Kip said. He paused for a moment, then asked, "Do you think that's it, that what she said is right?"

I turned to him. "Why not?"

"Nothing. I was just wondering how all that fitted into wanting or not wanting sex."

I looked at him. "I can't believe you're saying this."

"It's nothing, as long as you think it's true."

"What do you mean 'as long as *you* think it's true'?"

"Nothing! If you're happy with the explanation, then I am, too." He glanced over at me and almost ran a red light. He hit the brakes hard and we thunked forward. I ignored the jolt and kept right on arguing.

"What? It's not a question of being *happy* about it."

"So you feel unsafe with me?" Kip asked.

"Why else would I be like this? It's not physical. So it's got to be psychological, *okay*?" I turned away and stared out the window. Instead of feeling happy like I'd been when I bounced out of the therapist's office, I was now full of self-recrimination. "I really hate this part. I'm totally responsible for this."

I was also pissed at Kip. Why couldn't he just accept what Julie said? Why did he have to cast doubt on it? Kip must've read my thoughts because he reached over with one hand and put it over mine. "No, you're not. That's not what she meant," he said.

"It boils down to the same thing—it's all in my frickin' head."

"Look at it this way. It's a start. We're identifying the problem."

"Yeah, I suppose."

We drove on in silence.

Six

THE LOVE AND
SEX BANK

ater I happened to encounter Julie's emotional safety theory again in a book by Barbara DeAngelis: *What Women Want Men to Know*. DeAngelis said women need to feel *safe*—that is, loved and appreciated—in order to be open to arousal. Sounds simple, but once you read exactly what that takes, it's an almost impossible task. First, there are the usual things. For example, women like to be seduced, we hate to be rushed, and men better pay attention to that darn clit. Then we have the less tangible psychological needs: "Women need to be turned on in their hearts and heads first," writes DeAngelis. I'd heard that one before, too. But taking cues from DeAngelis about how to turn on women's hearts and minds could put Kip—or many a man, for that matter—on a wild goose chase.

BE PREPARED

DeAngelis says that for women to get into even a *preparatory* state in which a tiny thought of sexual desire may be introduced, they "need to be relaxed and free from distractions." And DeAngelis means any and all distractions. Even thinking, "Oh no, I forgot to call the dentist back" can derail a woman's desire right in the middle of sex, she says. That also includes any slight, no matter how apparently small, no matter if it occurred weeks ago, that your man may have unwittingly delivered. So necessary is a Zen state free from any anxiety and discontent to a woman's sexual arousal that DeAngelis counts anything that contributes to this state as "foreplay." So, apologizing for any slight she may feel he has dealt her, whether the result of her imagination or not, is foreplay. When a man does chores like taking out the garbage, it's foreplay. Changing the kitty litter is foreplay. Listening attentively to his wife's apprehensiveness about wearing a certain color dress at her second cousin's wedding is foreplay. Indulging her every mood or whim is foreplay. Reading about all the very, and I mean *very*, numerous things a man must be sensitive to in order for his wife or girlfriend to consider giving him even a yellow light made me shake my head. Be vewwy, vewwy good, and *maybe* I'll be in the mood for nooky.

DeAngelis is not alone. On *Oprah*, Dr. Laura Berman said, "A lot of men don't realize that some of the best foreplay you can give your wife is taking the kids, washing the dishes, cleaning up. She will be so turned on, right?" I'm seemingly alone in thinking that doing the dishes does not constitute foreplay. Around here, it's Kip, not me, who is the clean, tidy, organized one. I'm Oscar to his Felix. But watching him cleaning the house, doing the dishes, and paying the bills does not make me one bit hornier. Not a bit. By the same token, Kip's sex drive doesn't *decrease* just because I have left the dishes in the sink and the kitchen floor unmopped. I do think a guy who does household chores is more likely to get a thank-you boink—if he finishes them. That's the trick. Who can ever catch up on chores? Even so, watching Kip trying wouldn't increase my urge to have sex. Personally, I'd rather take him out for ice cream. But DeAngelis doesn't consider such first-get-the-chores-done "foreplay" as manipulation, barter, or excuse. It's Darwinian, primordial—scientific, really. Blame it on our ancestors.

DeAngelis believes women have evolved to include an area in their minds that she refers to as a "Love and Sex Bank." If a man doesn't deposit enough love into the bank, then she won't be able to withdraw any sexual feeling for him. "Often it's how you've been treating your partner for hours, days, even weeks before you approach her to make love that will determine whether or not she is in the mood." DeAngelis says women tally it all up, whether big or small, and then when a man wants sex, we determine whether he's welcome in our arms. DeAngelis personifies this mental calculation as "The Supervisor of Sex and Intimacy," a homunculus whose job it is "to decide if the information being received by the woman's nerve endings will get transferred on to the erogenous zones in the form of arousal or not." In one instance, the Supervisor may determine that Mr. Mister has been a bit neglectful this past week—no sex for you!

But a man shouldn't blame the Supervisor's decision on punitive calculation. That is, a woman isn't consciously refusing to be sexually aroused. The Supervisor of Sex and Intimacy is being protective rather than punitive. DeAngelis says the Supervisor is "the part of a woman who protects her from opening up sexually if she's not feeling safe." The Supervisor is an ancestral vestige handed down through the millennia to protect women from mating with any jerkface that might knock them up and leave.

Could be. But it's tough to see how not taking out the garbage and disagreeing about where to go on vacation could possibly be more than irritating. It may even be infuriating, but *safety* issues? Suddenly anything that might upset a woman is categorized as an emotional safety issue. Was there nothing that *wouldn't* be categorized as a safety issue?

I have to admit I was tempted to swallow DeAngelis's theory whole because all the reasons I told Kip why I didn't want sex were cataloged in her book. Not only that, she listed lots more than I could have thought of (her book might come in handy as a bedside reference). Most of all, I wanted to be able to say to myself: *See, you weren't giving* excuses *for not wanting sex—these are legitimate* reasons.

And I do think DeAngelis is right—we women do tally up every resentment and slight against us. But despite my need to be championed by DeAngelis, I had a nagging suspicion that the decision to refuse sex was a conscious and rational one rather than an unconscious and instinctual one, because in DeAngelis's book, new issues keep on popping up. I'm sure any man who had to keep up with it all, every detail that is part of daily life, would feel like he's playing Whack-a-Mole, trying feverishly to hammer problems as soon as they pop out of their holes. Once you recategorize any annoyances that plague your relationship, large or small, into safety issues, you create drama from even the most trivial.

And if there is anything I know about, it's how to make drama of the trivial. I am a drama queen. If something catastrophic is happening, I'm the calm one. But the lower an incident rates on the Richter scale, the more I go nuts. And since it's the smallish "challenges" that constitute most of life, I'm emotionally in deep doo-doo. I prefer to take out most of my frustrations, irritations, pouting, sniping, and various other forms of obnoxious behaviors on the one I love. Kip, bless his heart, takes them in stride and tries to do everything he can to comfort me and say "There-there, poor baby, it will all be all right." Okay, I admit I taught him the "there-there, poor baby" part. That's because he gives constructive advice when I'm venting and all I want is sympathy. But as far as reassuring me goes and being a rock—he's terrific. He's been my emotional rock through many a storm. But has this done anything to increase my desire for sex? In a word, no.

NO EXCUSES

I look down at DeAngelis's book. Her smiling face on the back is so gently reassuring. "It isn't you," it whispered. "It's that man in your life who can't understand the emotions, the thoughts, the *feelings* of a woman." As much as I wanted to believe that Kip was at fault for not anticipating every foul wind that might blow through my head, I knew he was always there for me. I took a deep breath and waved bye-bye to the emotional safety theory. DeAngelis was on the ship's bow, waving a handkerchief at me, yelling that there were no more reasons left and that this was my last chance to come on board. I turned my back and walked down the dock. What now? What now, indeed.

*K*ip had already had his solo session with Julie. "Well, are you going to tell me what she said?" Then I paused. "Or, do you want to keep it private?"

"No, that's okay." He said she asked if he had pressured me into sex, or demanded me to perform unwelcome sexual acts, or if I had any pain during intercourse. All to which Kip had correctly replied in the negative. She also asked him if I had always had a low desire for sex. That was an affirmative. Apparently, I was the problem child.

Still, I was willing to continue with Julie, even if it was for more meager straws to grasp onto. But after only a handful of sessions, I got a call from her office saying that she had a family emergency and would not be taking any appointments. I asked when she was getting back. There was silence, then the secretary said in a hushed, gossipy tone that Ms. Legs was getting a divorce and moving her practice back to Minneapolis. "Huh" was all I could come up with.

Ah, well, the therapy was getting us nothing but a diminished bank account anyway. Kip and I continued to have infrequent sex and a roller coaster of emotional tension in our relationship. But we managed to hang on to each other. We got married that winter, on a crackling cold day in December.

Seven

IN THE DRIVER'S SEAT

With Julie gone, I was thrown back on the women's magazines. The *Ladies' Home Journal* has a regular feature called "Can This Marriage Be Saved?" One issue featured a couple having problems in the bedroom. Patty doesn't want the amount or the kind of sex that her husband does—but she's been giving in out of guilt and fear. We are taken through the usual sordid mess that makes so many women squirm. The wife complains that her husband wants sex no matter the situation and she has given in countless times. They went through many bad patches in the marriage, but no matter what stress the couple was under, "it didn't do anything to slow down Sean's sex drive." Patty says, "If anything, Sean has become more sexually adventurous, always wanting to try new positions." But thanks to joint therapy addressing her husband's problem with aggression and her own problem with passive-aggressiveness, they're happy campers in the bedroom: "As Sean gradually toned down his temper, Patty became more comfortable speaking her mind. After a few months, she was able to report, 'I don't say yes to sex unless I'm really in the mood. Now, we make love a few times a week—and I'm often the one who initiates it!'" The usual fairy-tale ending to our sex fable.

A common narrative of the sexually unhappy couple starts with too much pressure for sex on one spouse's part (usually the husband). The relationship expert then tells said libidinous spouse to back off. He backs off, and lo and behold, the formerly sexually reluctant wife rewards him with an above-statistically-average amount of sex! Yes, if he had just let the sex thing ride from the beginning, she would have been only too eager to make love several times a week. Oh, the humorous irony. The more he pressed for sex, the less she wanted. The less he initiated sex, the more she wanted to have sex. Maybe. But it left me suspicious that the above scenario too easily resolved itself into a sustained sexual equilibrium.

The lesson is that sexual desire will naturally flourish as long as we give the low-desire partner a nurturing, unpressured environment. I didn't think much of this theory, but apparently Kip wanted to give it a whirl.

One day he came home after work and was unusually quiet. "What's up?" I said while emptying a bag of frozen dinner rolls into a dish.

"I don't know."

"Something's wrong. Tell me." I punched the defrost button on the microwave and then turned to look at him.

"I've been thinking that maybe it would be better if you're the one who initiates sex."

"Oh," I said. I wasn't prepared for a discussion of *that*. Why now? I don't like these surprises. The "oh" continued to hang in the air without follow-up. I didn't know if I wanted him to go on. It sounded like he was resigning himself to something. Given up on my ever showing him any sexual enthusiasm.

"Then I'd know you were having sex only when you really wanted to."

"Oh."

"Well . . . ? What do you think?"

My brain was flooded with all sorts of thinks. Thoughts flew back and forth like pinballs. First I wondered if this was some kind of trick or a test. He's going to gauge my sexual feelings for him by how often I initiate sex. Shit. I know where that leads. I remember the women on *Oprah*. Husbands saying to their wives that they weren't in a real marriage if they didn't have sex so many times a month. You were just roommates, then. That's the death knell, isn't it? But at the same time, one part of me was elated. No more pressure or guilt. I wouldn't have to pretend to be too busy, too sleepy, or too aggravated to have sex. Freedom! Then again, what if I hardly initiated sex at all? What if I became complacent? I already had two pairs of flannel pajamas. I'll end up sitting in my pj's, eating a pan of brownies and watching reruns of *Mary Tyler Moore* on TV-Land. *Who can turn the world on with her smile?* Apparently, not me. All of these thoughts were shooting through my mind at warp speed. The bottom line is that I wasn't prepared to shoulder the responsibility for our sex life.

"Look," Kip said. "I don't want to have to keep guessing if you're really in the mood or not. I don't want you to have sex with me out of guilt."

"Sure. Sure." I felt cornered. I needed time to think, time to absorb all this.

"Well?" When Kip still got no answer, he stretched his arms up and out in a gesture of *what gives?*

"Yeah, we could do it that way. It's an idea." I was looking down at the kitchen floor, rubbing my toe over a small piece of lettuce that had fallen there.

"What? Is that it? Anything else?" He knew I was hedging.

"Yeah, well, no. I mean it's an idea. It's a *good* idea. We'll see how it plays out." I willed myself to look up—to look sincere and not nervous.

Kip left the kitchen and I stooped down to pick up the shriveled lettuce. I stared at it like it was the only thing left that made sense in the world. I was conscious of the fact that Kip and I might be stepping over a new threshold in our marriage. I walked over to the garbage can, pressed my foot on the lever, and flicked the lettuce into the basket. I thought, what if this were the top of the slide, and we were about to go swiftly down? I leaned back on the counter and pinched the bridge of my nose, trying to stave off tears. It felt like my marriage was dying. God, I hated this. I hated being like this. I wanted my crisis cigarette. I'd all but quit cigarettes three years earlier, but every couple of months or so, I'd have one when I thought I was going over the edge. But I didn't want Kip to see how desperate I felt at this moment. I didn't want him to think that I thought this was the end.

Kip had told me, as he'd told me before, that he wouldn't leave me over sex—he just wanted me to be straight about what to expect. And he wanted me to be honest about my desire. Yet even so, I played head games with myself. I didn't want him to think that left to my own devices, I could go without sex *forever*. I was very appreciative that he was leaving sex up to me. But now that he had, how else was I to show my gratitude to him backing off of sex than to reward him with . . . sex! That was the paradox. Now that he was leaving our sex life up to me, I had to prove that he had left it in capable hands—that he hadn't just handed it over to someone who was going to neglect it and let it die. If this was a test, I wasn't going to pass. I knew my husband thought he'd been fooled and putting the ball in my court would prove it.

Eight

QUICKIES

The burden of shouldering our sex life was always in the back of my mind. And there it was, weighing on me as I went to meet my friend Diane downtown one Saturday. Cleveland is always freezing in February and the wind whipped down the streets, moving powdery snow in waves along the sidewalk. Aargh! Why did I agree to go out? This was *not* invigorating. I shuffled along in my overcoat, tucking my chin like a turtle into the seven-foot-long scarf that I could have wrapped ten times around my neck if I'd wanted to. I pulled my knit hat lower on my head, almost covering my eyes.

I clapped my hands together as I waited for Diane outside of May's. There was at least some shelter from the wind there. But I really didn't take much advantage of it because I was so impatient and had to keep peeking around the corner of the building to see if I could see her bus coming. Every time I did that, the wind would blast my face with pins and needles. I'd go back around the corner, stamp my booted feet, and then repeat the process for the umpteenth time. Finally I saw the 326 bus three blocks down. Should be here in a minute.

When the bus arrived and Diane stepped off, we immediately went into the Terminal Tower to warm up. We toured some of the shops there, but staying inside was not what we'd had in mind when we decided to go downtown. Happily, the sun came out and the wind died down enough for us to push through the revolving doors to the outside. We went for a walk along Euclid Avenue. As we strolled, I summoned up the courage to confide my rocky relationship with Kip to my friend.

"I wonder if I'm avoiding sex with Kip," I said, not really wondering at all. "He gets so pissy when I tell him that hey, it's been a hard day, I need to unwind (if I can), and then, I hope, get a solid night's sleep. When he wants sex in the middle of the damn week, it drives me crazy. I know we're supposed to have sex two-point-five times a week, but I can't do it. I just can't."

"What about the weekends?" Diane asked. "Do you get your two-point-five in then? Because then he doesn't have *annnny* reason to complain."

"Well . . ." I wasn't sure how much I wanted to divulge. It was embarrassing. "Not . . . exactly. I can't make up for a week's worth of sex in couple of days. Well, technically, three nights. I mean there's Friday night, and I'm still wiped from the day. And Sunday night . . . who wants to do it Sunday night? I'm trying to cram my last precious hours of relaxation in before Monday. I hate Mondays with a passion." I furrowed my brow just *thinking* of Mondays but realized I was getting off topic. "So that leaves only Saturday, really. I mean, if you want good-quality sex, then Saturday's it. But Kip does have to work every other Saturday night . . ."

"Hmm."

She was probably hiding a smirk behind that neutral face. I rushed on. "I know, that sounds bad, like I'm making excuses." I pulled down my scarf and looked at her. "Do you think I'm making excuses?"

"Maybe. But no more than I do. In some ways, I'm even worse. I want to hoard the entire weekend to myself. I almost always only have sex with Rick during the week. Quickie stuff. That way I get it all out the way so that I can *enjoy* my weekends."

"Huh," I said. Where I procrastinated, she got it out of the way. Now that was smart. But, more important, Diane was like me—another sex avoider. I had a partner in crime. So, I told her how relieved I was that I wasn't the only one who dreaded sex.

"Oh, no. It's a chore, like anything else."

"But you're brilliant. You get it out of the way so you don't have to feel guilty about it and Rick stays happy as a clam."

"Yeah, but that doesn't mean he doesn't want weekend sex. He does."

We crossed busy Euclid Avenue. More people appeared on the walk now that the sun was shining, and we were carried along by the crowd. The smell of hot cashews drifted out from The Nuthouse. We inhaled deeply, but then headed over to the hot-dog vendors. Diane bought a plain hot dog while I ordered a Polish boy with ketchup and kraut.

I go to only two hot-dog vendors in downtown: a little, wiry, middle-aged woman, because she looks the least scary (nonetheless, all the hot-dog vendors have been cited for unsanitary carts), and Floyd. He set his cart in front of Brother's Printing, just across from the concrete prison known as Cleveland State University. Floyd was a short guy with long, frizzy black hair. He wore leather wristbands and had one very long fingernail that he painted black and red with a glued-on sequin. He played in a punk band that I saw once and hated. But when I bought stuff from Floyd, I felt like I was supporting the underground culture.

Munching on her hot dog, Diane told me how she avoided weekend sex. "I always pull the same thing. I think he's onto me, but he's not going to rock the boat by calling me on it. At least not yet—and it's been years."

Diane showed me how she does it. She breathed slowly, heavily. She said, "I shut my eyes, but not too tightly. Very relaxed, very languid. I've got it down." On weekend mornings, she could never seem to rouse herself until after her husband had gotten up and was making himself breakfast. "I toss and turn when he nudges me playfully, trying to get me to wake up. But I push his arm away while mumbling something incoherent as if I'm still in a half-unconscious state. Sometimes it takes him so damn long to get going and get out of the bedroom. He dawdles until I want to scream, 'C'mon, get up. Get those Wheaties!' "

She suspected that her husband cleared his throat and lumbered around in the hope that it would wake her. "No such luck," she said to me. "I know it sounds mean. He is such a sweet guy and here I am mentally shoving him across the floor and out the bedroom door like a linebacker at the fifty-yard line."

She pantomimed by lunging forward on one leg with her arms straight out in front of her, pushing the air, then putting her shoulder into it, adding a few grunts for dramatic flair. "See," she said, straightening up and turning toward me with a grin, "Ain't I just awful?"

"No, I *totally* understand. I do!" I bent over and started laughing, bits of hot-dog bun flying out of my mouth.

iane swore by John Gray's chapter on quickies. "Read it. Really," she said, "You'll love it." Kip was out seeing *Spider-Man* part-something. So I had most of the evening to myself. I got into my robe and slippers and grabbed some Ben & Jerry's. I lugged *Mars and Venus in the Bedroom* onto my lap for a closer study. It's always in print, so I thought there's got to be a reason Gray's book is a perennial favorite. Just maybe he could be my new pal.

WHEN MARS MEETS VENUS

Gray starts out explaining the difference between the sex drives of men and women by appealing to metaphor, saying that men are like the sun, having a defined time for rising and setting (translation: guys know right off the bat whether they're in the mood for sex or not) while women are more like the moon, going through various phases (that is, we have less on-or-off certainty about our sexual desire). It's particularly hard because, according to Gray, women themselves often don't know if they want sex. Gray says, "Many times a woman is potentially in the mood for sex but a man just doesn't realize it." In the next sentence he says that this can lead a man to feel "rejected when she might really want sex." In other words, a man may be needlessly going through the frustration of being sexually rejected by his wife simply because she can't discern whether or not she wanted sex.

This is what confused me: Gray said, if the man is the first to inquire, "Would you like to have sex?" or "Are you in the mood for sex?" and the women responds with an "I don't know" or an "I'm not sure," he should *not* take those responses as a polite way of saying no. Instead, he should follow up with the question "Is there a part of you that wants to have sex with me?" Gray says, "Almost always she will say yes." *Of course* she's almost always going to say yes. What woman would say, *There is no part of me that wants to have sex with you?* I couldn't. Which is the point of the wording of that question. It makes it impossible to say no to sex without it coming off as a personal insult. Gray hides the fact that the question itself is deliberately manipulative in the lowest sense—preying on the fact that most women don't want to globally reject their husband. I had a feeling that this man would not be my new pal.

Gray adds that if the wife then starts launching into how tough a day she's had, or how tired she is, or why her mood is yucky (which Gray warns might happen), the man should not take it to mean that she doesn't want to have sex with him. She's only venting. She just needs someone to listen to her frustrations. And ergo, if he proves himself to be a good listener, she just might show her appreciation. Because, as I learned from every damn talk show and self-help book, the ultimate, weeping joy of a woman is a man who is a good listener. If he listens attentively to her whining as to why sex doesn't sound appealing right now, he might get her to change her mind or she'll change her own mind. To Gray, this is proof positive that women often don't know if they do want sex.

I had an alternative explanation. It's not because he's a good listener that puts her in the mood. It's guilt. After a woman goes through her elaborate justification for not being in the mood as he gazes at her sympathetically, she's going to feel like the whining idiot she is. She knows she wants to get out of sex. And here he is lovingly looking at her like a lapdog and she's chastising herself for thinking, *Yes, of course honey, I wish a part of me did want to have sex with you. And if it weren't for all these rotten excuses I'm giving you that imply my emotional reactions to petty everyday troubles eclipse any desire I might have for you, I would be able to give you a clear, un-guilty, straightforward no. But here you are being such a good listener. A godsend. The least I can do is fuck you.*

Gray has us deal in old-fashioned sophomoric male manipulation and pressure: "C'mon, Babycakes, what's wrong?" And Babycakes says, "I dunno," to which her man says, "Aww, Babycakes, tell me all about it and then I can kiss it and make it all better. You just don't know what you want, do you?" But even if Babycakes still doesn't warm to his kindly ministrations, he can always make a last-ditch plea: "How about a quickie?"

BE QUICK ABOUT IT

Ah, the quickie. It has an important place in Gray's book. A quickie is the stopgap covering the distance between a man's desire and a woman's. Gray addresses the issue head-on. He knows that great sex for women won't necessarily increase the frequency with which they'll crave sex, at least not substantially enough to match a man, which is why he has a twenty-page chapter titled "The Joy of Quickies." When a woman doesn't want sex, instead of saying no to her man, she can offer him a quickie. He gets off, and she doesn't have to perform or take more than ten minutes out of her day.

Gray is gracious enough to give the little woman a sample script she can work from when hubby starts humping her leg while she's washing the dishes. He says, "By making quickies guilt free, a woman automatically supports a man in feeling free to initiate sex. These are some common phrases for initiating sex and common answers a woman can give instead of saying no":

- "He says, 'I'm feeling really turned on to you. Let's have sex.'
   "She says, 'I'm not in the mood for sex, but we could have a quickie.'
- "He says, 'I've missed you. Let's find some time to have sex.'
   "She says, 'Um, that sounds like a good idea. I don't have a lot of time right now, but we could have a quickie.'
- "He says, 'Let's have sex tonight.'
   "She says, 'I really got a bad headache. Maybe we could have sex tomorrow. I could give you a hand job right now.'
- "He says nothing but gently reaches over in bed and begins making the moves.
   "She whispers, 'Um, this feels good. Don't worry about me tonight. Just go for it.' "

There is really no reason to tell your man no. Instead of saying no, just say yes to a quickie. Even if you have a bastard of a headache, tell your husband he can get a hand job out of you.

A QUICK GIFT

Though I don't agree with Gray's philosophy on quickies, or maybe it's just his attitude, Diane did find them useful. She initiated quickies a couple of times a week as a preemptive strike against her husband's initiations, which could result in far longer or more complicated sex sessions. She'd hop on him, do her thing, and pretend to have an orgasm early (although most of the time she didn't). Then, "exhausted," she'd collapse on the bed. Diane-style quickies—now this was something I could do. No sweat. After all, Gray assured me that Kip was secretly longing for it:

> *Although most men are happy to please their partners, sometimes a man can feel that he just wants to skip all the foreplay and, as the slogan goes, just do it. Something deep inside him wants to cut loose and completely let go without any restraint or worry about lasting longer or what he should do to make his partner happy.*

Now, this to me is perfectly understandable. Since Gray teaches couples that women do need a good long warm-up before intercourse, it seems only fair that sometimes a guy just wants to cut loose and zoom, zoom, zoom. It is especially fair in light of the fact that according to Gray, when a woman *does* want sex, a man should do a *lot* of work in getting her to the proper level of excitation.

For instance, he tells men that in order to get their wives properly aroused, they should be prepared to "camp out" between her legs for up to twenty minutes or so of cunnilingus. That's a long time. (Let me make a long aside here. I must ruefully confess: I do *not* like the idea of a man camping out between my legs. And as a woman, I'm supposed to absolutely go zonkers over it. Kip likes it, but for me, at best, it tickles. I'm sure if I let Kip go on and on, I'd probably have an orgasm. But that would be a reflex. And I'd be too grossed out along the way to want a repeat. I keep seeing two dogs licking each other's crotch. Or maybe the trauma came from dogs trying to lick *my* crotch. And to top it off, I've got this theory that oral sex can cause yeast infections. I think the tongue has tons more germs than a vagina and I don't want it in the neighborhood. My vagina would be defenseless against the onslaught of microbes.) But it could be said that if a guy does pop his pup tent and give cunnilingus to a woman for a good twenty minutes, and regularly follows *Mars and Venus*'s other techniques for his wife's increased pleasure, he may deserve an occasional day off for an effortless quickie.

Gray says that if a woman does agree to a quickie, it should be acknowledged that this is her "gift" to him. That's because the quickie includes no foreplay and lasts only a few minutes; thus women are not expected to get as much pleasure from it.

Yet Gray states that women sometimes will actually *prefer* a quickie—even in lieu of extended foreplay. It's an assertion that goes against the prevailing notion that women will always vote for extended foreplay over a quick roll the hay. And it contradicts Gray's former assertion that women love our lovemaking long and slow. But Gray's other observation is that often women don't want sex as much as men. I thought, *Yeah, Gray, something we both agree on!* He said though women prefer lengthy foreplay when they do desire sex, they'd prefer the sex be short and sweet when they're not in the mood. So true again! Except for the lengthy foreplay. I don't like lengthy foreplay. I have too much time to think, and if I think, that's it. I'm out of the mood. Unless lengthy foreplay means lobster down at Don's Lighthouse Bar & Grill. Buy me a fancy dinner and I'm your good-time girl. Just kidding. Maybe.

Whatever, it comes down to this: Gray's telling me if I'm willing to accommodate my husband every time he wants sex, then I shouldn't have to be stressed about performing and responding on top of it. The easier a man makes it for a woman, the more she'll be willing to have sex with her mate during those times she doesn't want sex.

Lying there like a log while your guy heaves up and down on you sounds humiliating. But in all honesty, how many of us would like this option available? A short blow job that doesn't cramp your jaw. A hand job. More times than we care to admit, we'd be delighted if our men would just hop in the saddle for a few minutes (only!) while we did absolutely nothing and then *boom*—it's over. Responding can take a lot of work, whereas while just lying there, one can presumably make out the grocery list or figure out how adding energy to an accelerating object affects its gravitational mass. He gets his sex quota in and you don't have to feel guilty.

EFFORTLESS SEX?

Pam Lister, a former editor at *Redbook* and author of *Married Lust,* joins the chorus on the virtues of the quickie: "The value of sex sometimes is simply in the connection. Period. And what your husband reads into your willingness to be spontaneous and go with the moment is that you want him under any condition, good, bad, and indifferent." That's nice, but I *don't* want to have sex with Kip under *any* condition, especially that second one—bad. I'm thinking what might a "bad condition" entail? I suspect she means bad for the woman—like Gray and the bastard headache. And what is Lister getting at when she says that sometimes the value of sex is just the connection? Does that mean desire for sex isn't necessary? Lister doesn't give us time to dwell on this thought. She quickly runs us through to all the great things a quickie can do for you.

According to Lister, quickie sex, in many senses, doesn't *count* as real sex for women, but the great thing is that it counts for men. Lister says that with a quickie, "You don't have to worry about pleasuring him; the immediacy of a quickie basically means he's got to take his own pleasure, which is a huge relief if you're feeling overwhelmed by responsibility everywhere else." A quickie is supposedly so effortless that for the woman, it's like not having sex at all. *Is this possible?* I absolutely wanted it to be.

HURRY IT UP, *PLEASE*

Well, that wasn't true for me. As far as me and Kip went, quickies turned out to take longer than the supposed five to seven minutes. That's because my husband was oblivious to the subtle demarcation that separated sex from a quickie. I was confused, too. What should I say if it's taking longer than anticipated? Do I say, *Okay, mister, time's up?* Clear my throat? Have a sneezing fit? How was I expected to handle it? Wouldn't saying or signaling time's up destroy all appearance that I find this anything but an unpleasant chore?

There's also another problem. The agreement is that a woman doesn't have to respond at all during a quickie or fake enjoyment. Maybe it was just me, but even with quickie sex—oops, don't call it *sex*—even with a quickie isn't there at least some pretense of enjoyment on the wife's part, no matter how small? Since I love to do role reversals, I imagined that I want to go dancing most nights of the week and Kip wants to stay home most nights of the week. He agrees to go on the condition that he just passively stands there while I push him around. Even if I had a couples' counselor to help me rationalize the whole thing, I'd still be looking for some sort of response of enjoyment or enthusiasm.

Wouldn't most men be searching out a positive reaction in their wives and girlfriends, too—despite insisting that they are just fine without one? And what would I think of any man who truly, *truly* didn't care if I was having an enjoyable time or not?

Adding more unwritten rules to the game, what woman wouldn't try to hurry along a quickie that threatens to go into overtime by faking enjoyment?

I worry about these technicalities because they're important. The devil is in the details and things that sound good in books may break down in practical application. From experience I've learned that, absent my own sexual desire, quickies are seldom the neutral, quick, and effortless experience Gray or Lister presents them to be. It's not anyone's fault really. Sex isn't like a well-choreographed dance.

I even have difficulty with the purist quickies, the kind that should supposedly require little more from me than my presence. The reason these can still go bad is that the quickie has male orgasm as its goal. That means that despite all the lovely talk of quickies being a snap, the male orgasm is still in the driver's seat. I'm given to understand that the goal of quickies is to satisfy men without taxing women. But sometimes these twin aims work against each other's interest. If I count an orgasm as generally synonymous with male sexual satisfaction, then a quickie that doesn't result in his orgasm is worthless. Maybe even worse than worthless. It then becomes my mission to get him to orgasm. My attitude is that since I've already invested so much time and effort into a sexual act I don't desire, it better damn well be worth it to one of us.

Nine

SPONTANEITY

I'll admit, treating Kip like a car at Jiffy Lube revealed my crummy attitude. But I was desperate. Maybe, I thought, the problem is that I keep focusing on *my* feelings instead of my husband's. Lister, who seems to be taking a few cues from Gray, thinks that a woman should be happy by making her man sexually happy. When a woman gives too much weight to her own feelings, she might just skip sex until she does feel like having it. Lister poses this question to her readers in *Married Lust:* "But what if you don't feel like it? If you don't, you don't. So be it. But as anyone who's been a woman long enough will tell you, it's plain dumb to postpone sex until you feel like it . . ." Why is it plain dumb? Because, Lister says, there are so many other things competing for your time and attention, you may never get around to sex. But a woman can take advantage of spontaneous opportunities to squeeze in sex. She gives an instance of a husband and wife who had refrained from sex during the last month of her pregnancy and were "chomping on the bit" for sex:

> *Finally, after a not-too-difficult delivery, when the doctors and nurses finally left the room and the baby was safely tucked away in the nursery, this woman gave her husband a big kiss, and as she put it, "Got right down off the bed and gave him some." Now, I'm not exactly sure what she gave him. The point isn't what she did, but that she did it. Do you think her husband will ever, ever forget that? Not a chance.*

Lister has the good sense to know how this will play to her audience: "Now you can say, ewww, how politically incorrect, how over-the-top a man-pleasing move that was. But who's to say?" Well, who *is* to say? Let none of us be in a rush to judgment of any of our fellow human beings. But if you have chosen this example as a lesson to us all on wifely devotion, please allow us to form an opinion, judgmental as it may be. Lister has formed her opinion, and she acknowledges that it may not be to a lot of folks' taste, however: "This woman saw an opportunity to show her love, and turned a small moment in time into an intimate memory that would tide them over as a couple through the difficult months ahead." I suppose the memory of his wife giving him "some" within a couple of hours of giving childbirth does graphically display that his needs take priority, in her mind to her own. And apparently, he was happy to accept her loving gift somewhere in the vicinity of the hospital bed and the floor.

Though some of us may find this new mother's actions extreme,

Lister says, "Personally, I had to hand it to her for understanding and acting on the basic principle of sexual spontaneity: When the moment's right, you go for it, whether you're driven by love, charity, magnanimity, hormones, or the full moon." Lister has revamped what most of us had thought as sexual spontaneity; namely, that if you're both horny and a time or a place suddenly comes up where you can act on it, *boom!* Instead, Lister takes out the need for sexual feelings. A woman need not feel in the mood for sex to take advantage of a sexual opportunity. That is, the desire for sex is not a prerequisite for surprising her husband with "some." Love, charity, magnanimity, whatever.

Well, men may like big, sexy surprises, but I don't. To wit: the day when Kip surprised *me* with "some." Though extraordinarily tame and dull by the above standard (no IV drip was involved), my most memorable instance of spontaneous sex was that wet and steamy classic, the morning shower: I was taking a shower when in walked Kip, looking for a good time. He stepped into the shower and immediately started howling. He wasn't used to the Dante-like temperature I always keep my showers at. He quickly reached for the cold handle and turned it way up. That pissed me off. I don't like compromising on my personal shower time. But there he was, taking that risk and making a foray into the land of spontaneous quickies. That was a big step for us. So I figured I'd work with it. But I was about to find that sex in the shower is not as romantic and sensual as it sounds. It's like climbing a slippery, wet mountain. I had to balance, brace, and leverage myself against fixtures whose original purpose was decidedly hostile to spontaneous sexual antics. Clinging to the grout between the tiles with my fingernails was not my idea of a good time. Kip loved it. I hated it, but kept my mouth shut—followed by increasingly weird explanations as to why we should never shower together again. I believe the danger of invisible toenail fungus was mentioned.

Women of the new millennium are *supposed* to enjoy sex. Sex is healthy. Sex is good. Sex is what keeps passion alive. Sex is what keeps love alive. Sex is what makes us feel alive. But then there's the shame; more often than we're comfortable with, we fake enjoying sex to protect Tom, Dick, or Harry's ego. But that's not the only reason.

Another reason to have unwanted sex is that your husband might be thinking about suitcases. The sexperts rarely address it, but it's an ugly truth that women who choose to stay home with their children or work part-time are afraid of sliding into poverty without their husband's full income. Many women are in fear of their husband leaving the marriage if they don't kick up the sex quotient. Combine that with a culture that gives approbation to the ideal of the libidinous woman and pathologizes the rest of us, and we have men with the means and the reason to leave their "undersexed" wives. On the other hand, men don't fear their wives leaving them over *too* much sex. No such animal. That's why women are haunting the self-help section of bookstores, why we tune in to *Oprah,* why we watch the Bermans and take notes. *Fear.*

I want to believe we're not like our grandmothers or great-great-grandmothers, who were taught that sex, though unpleasant, was part of the business of marriage. Isn't that the mentality that I was trying to escape by rationalizing unwanted sex into a gift? But I know now that's only a temporary fix. If you don't enjoy sex, and are having it anyway, you are truly being submissive in the most personal way possible.

Ten

WOULD ORGASMS
DO THE TRICK?

*Y*ou seemed to be really enjoying yourself."

I knew what he was after. I also knew he would not push it so hard as to directly ask me if I had had an orgasm. We both knew enough from the sexperts everywhere in the media that one shouldn't pressure the other person by keeping score. That would just trivialize the rest of the sex experience and make for disappointment and guilt. Thus I used the etiquette of don't ask, don't tell.

I'd say, "Oh, I had a very nice time indeed," in a tone that said I was making a playfully wild underestimate.

Kip would smile in satisfaction. "I could tell."

DEMANDING ORGASMS

But Marcia and Lisa Douglass, authors of *Are We Having Fun Yet?*, say it's not all right for women *not* to have orgasms. Orgasms are an important factor in making sex enjoyable. The Douglasses point out that no one would sanction the same notion turned around on men: that men can be just as fulfilled without orgasm. So, it's not all right lying there and saying, *It's okay honey, I just like being close to you.* It's not all right to give in to an act that uses you as a tool for some-one else's pleasure. That's why the sisters Douglass are up in arms about Gray's notion of a good time—because he blithely disregards what joyless sex can mean to a woman over time. (And there is something about Gray's soft, lubricious arrogance that makes you want to smother him with a pillow.)

For Douglass and Douglass, the problem stems not from bio-chemical or psychological differences between men and women, but from their anatomical differences. In support of their point, the authors note that most women do come every time they mastur-bate. We know how to hit the right spots every time. We know how long to spend in this or that area. The right amount of pressure. The right type of motion. This leads the Douglasses to conclude that women can easily have orgasms when physically stimulated correctly. When women masturbate, orgasms are not elusive. If a man could understand and become skilled in the ways that stimu-late his partner to orgasm—then logically, she would climax nearly every time they had sex together. And with the consistent physical gratification that orgasm can bring, women are going to desire more sex. Orgasm is the incentive.

I had to admit Douglass and Douglass made a powerful case.

If women are having orgasms when they masturbate, why aren't they having orgasms just as often when they engage in partner sex? This seems to disprove the idea that women are naturally less orgasmic than men. Then why aren't we having orgasms during sex? Simply put, the authors think that with the right mixture of manual, oral, and penile stimulation, women can have orgasms as often as they do when they masturbate. Sex, according to them, is foremost a skill.

I PREFER TO TANGO ALONE

The Douglasses' contention that if women can masturbate to orgasm then there is no justification whatsoever to claim that women are less orgasmic than men is a stunner. What do I say to that?

Okay, I had to scratch my head with this one, because, uh, from personal experience, I would say they're right. It is time for the author to reveal that she herself has bowed her own violin, and darned if she can't get her own strings to sing like Pavarotti. Moreover, though women tend to want less sex with their boyfriend, fiancé, or husband when going through a stressful time, they may actually masturbate *more*. One survey noted that women cite masturbating as an aid in going to sleep—obviously as stress relief—the same as men do.

However, women are far less likely to use sex *with a partner* as stress relief. If anything, sex with a man is stressful in and of itself and can lead to more or continued stress. I know; it shouldn't be like that. But it is. Regardless, I believe that women's lower libidos can account for the paradox of masturbation cohabiting with so-called frigidity.

For me, it had always gone something like this: Unless sexual satisfaction is easy to achieve, I'll pass, thank you very much. Unless I'm feeling particularly energetic or particularly horny, I'm not going to go out of my way—that is, not beyond my own manual resources. It would mean that I have to deal with someone else and their urges, and frankly, that's enough to deflate my meager libido. I don't want sex so much that I'd willingly involve another person. Why? Because my libido is just not very strong. It's as fickle as hell, it's apathetic, and it's not easily aroused or easily sustained. It isn't as if I'm never in the mood, but that I'm *seldom* in a mood *strong* enough to inspire my faith and confidence that it will carry me through sex with a partner like a good soldier and not desert me at some crucial point.

I approached sex like it was a boxing match. I'd throw a few fake punches in front of the mirror and dance around on my feet—yeah, feeling good, feeling fit, feeling sexy, feeling horny—trying exhaustively to turn my mood into real lust. But that put too much pressure on. Then I'd try not to think about how lusty I was or was not feeling, but that didn't work either. And on and on ad nauseam.

It's a lot of mental deceptions and counterdeceptions. I try to have a quiet mind and not become distracted by my thoughts. Even if I could allow myself to become sexually aroused in a relaxed, nonjudgmental way, that other adult squirming around breaks my concentration. My libido can't take distractions, or it just walks off, leaving my body as passionless as a dead trout.

More often than I'd like to admit, I treat sex as if I'm catering a party. No, I'm not a doormat; I'm a welcome mat. In hostess mode, I can't enjoy the party; I'm too worried about how the guests are doing. I go into hostess mode because, usually, sex is to please *him*. It's analogous to serving snacks during a football game. If you're not into football itself, you'll just spend time worrying if everyone else is enjoying themselves. And often, having sex is not to please me.

The truth is, unlike the women of *Sex and the City,* I don't spend my days looking for an opportunity to be pleased sexually by men. I *know* I'm supposed to be a little more selfish about my own sexual pleasure. I'm not afraid to give instructions. But I've found it's not about learning to be selfish, consciousness-raising, or grabbing the Dew. I know I *deserve* pleasure. But I'd just prefer to have it in another form—a back massage, a long bath, a caramel flan, or a good book. Sex, especially with a partner, is not something I frequently have a great urge for—not something I jump up and down just thinking about. On the contrary, often I have to try hard to work up enthusiasm for sex, but that's not for my sake, it's for Kip's.

LUST BY ORGASM

The Douglasses believe if women could reach orgasm as regularly during partner sex as they do during masturbation, then they would certainly want and even crave more sex with their partners. But for one of Patricia Love's clients, Pamela, reliable orgasms hadn't increased her desire for sex.

Dr. Love says Pamela and Dan are one couple for whom her orgasm isn't an issue, but her desire for sex is. Pamela says to Dan that she has little *spontaneous* interest in sex: "To be honest, I think if it weren't for pressure from you, I could go for a week without having one sexy thought. You initiate sex when your level of desire builds up; I initiate sex when my level of guilt builds up." For many women, the greatest aphrodisiac on a woman's libido isn't lust, it's guilt. What's unusual about this couple is that Pamela has orgasms

nearly every time she has intercourse with Dan, *without* direct cli-
toral stimulation. This makes her a rare bird indeed, according to
Love. Yet Pamela's desire for sex is not directly related to her ability
to have orgasms during sex. Pamela's explanation is one all of us
can understand. Even an orgasm just isn't worth the trouble:

> *For the first fifteen or twenty minutes of lovemaking I*
> *could happily stop at any point. I have hardly any sensation.*
> *It's only when my orgasm is imminent that I begin to feel*
> *horny. Then, all of a sudden, I'm thinking, "Don't stop! Don't*
> *stop!" But I crave sex for only about two minutes out of*
> *twenty. The rest of the time I could take it or leave it.*

The fact is that I can have orgasms—though not nearly as often
as I'd like. But even when I do, I must shamefacedly admit that the
effort Kip and I put in to getting me there is exhausting. Even when
one achieves the Holy Grail of orgasm with a partner, the effort
many women put forth is often great, though one feels an amazing
relief at having achieved it without having to fake or lie about it.
My chief hope was that Kip climaxed and I climaxed and I could
proudly give out blue ribbons and applause all the way around.

EXHAUSTED BY TRYING

I'm caught between these two philosophies of sex, the Douglasses'
and Gray's. Hmm, which path should I go down? Climb that mountain and keep striving for that orgasm? Or just relax and think, *If it*
happens, fine, if it doesn't, that's cool, too, because I'm still benefiting
my marriage?

But the philosophy of not striving for an orgasm is a little sneaky because of its goal. The theory is that if you don't pressure yourself to have an orgasm, you're more likely to have one. But whatever way I choose to go, it always ends up the same way; sometimes I have an orgasm and sometimes I don't.

And mostly, having an orgasm doesn't make me any more eager to have sex the next day—or the next week, for that matter. There has never been an appreciable, sustained effect.

"How was it?" asks Kip.

I know what he means. Did I come this time? I don't have the heart to tell him, *I don't care, I'm too exhausted to think about it.*

Eleven

THINKING
NAUGHTY THOUGHTS

I was ready to throw in the towel, but I looked in the mirror and told myself, *You just gotta suck it up.* There had to be a way that I could dig deeper into myself and find something that added up to more than the mere dutiful. *Cosmopolitan* did a feature on thinking naughty thoughts. Judging by not a few women's magazines, it's one popular, not to mention supercool way to set fire to your libido. I learned naughtiness is not limited to stealing your boss's coke stash. It's Benny Hill naughtiness. It's a French maid bending over to dust and, oopsy, forgetting that she forgot her underwear. It's doing the shoulder shimmy behind the back of any man who's under eighty and makes over ninety for the benefit of your girlfriends. Yummy, a real hottie.

I told Kip about this technique to get me to think about sex all day so that by the time he came home from work, I'd be horny as all get out. Kip said he'd be curious to see how it would go. I said I'd start tomorrow. Kip came home the next evening. We sat down to dinner and then watched the evening news. Kip turned to me and asked if I'd done any dirty thinking. I said no, I had forgotten all about it. "Remind me tomorrow morning, will ya?"

"Okay, if I remember," he said.

The next morning Kip had left a sticky on the bathroom mirror with two words and an exclamation mark: *Naughty Thoughts!*

That evening he asked, "Did you remember today?"

"Huh? Remember what?"

"The naughty thoughts."

I slapped the table with my hand, "Damn, I forgot *again!*"

"Now there's a prime example of the difference between men and women. I don't have to remember to have naughty thoughts— I've got them pretty much all day. It's hard for me *not* to think them," he said.

I racked my brain for naughty thoughts. I became hypervigilant to men on the street. I was like a sniper, scoping out hidden prey. I still had a lack of naughty thoughts. I believe I'm too picky about good-looking men. Well, I've seen them, but none have inspired anything more than, *Mmmm, very nice.* And not his butt. Just, very nice. I've only had true naughty thoughts—oh, dear—I am so quickly wearing of calling them naughty—about one guy. Mel Gibson as Mad Max. Yeah, when he was wearing tight black leather and had sidearms strapped to his thighs. Racking my brain some more—*um, oh, gosh, who else?* A Native American man in a sleeveless, ribbed T-shirt, with long, long black hair. That's it. Now, I *have* seen men that put major butterflies in my stomach. But I wasn't thinking of seeing them naked. No, they were more like little crushes. Forcing myself to think of men's butts and schlongs, or whatever, took, in fact, the attraction away for me.

There are other oddballs like me. Standing in line behind a pair of young women at Blockbuster, I heard one ask the other what she thought of Brad Pitt. The gist of the conversation was whether he wore boxers or tighty-whities. The one young woman said to the other that she loved Pitt, but wouldn't want to see him stripped down to his underwear. I know what she meant. Exactly.

TALK DIRTY TO ME

Thus, let me say that thinking naughty thoughts didn't come easily to me. I just knew I wasn't a naughty-thought thinker. It takes practice, sexperts like Laura Corn says. Naughty thoughts are especially effective when they occur in inappropriate settings. For instance, you are at a dinner party with your husband or boyfriend. You go up to him and whisper all the things you want to do to him when you get home. Then he whispers the same to you. And because you can't do anything right there and then, the waiting will inflame you both with desire. Corn says that by the end of the evening you'll both be desperate to rip the clothes off each other. I was more than leery about this advice. It might work for Kip, in fact I was pretty sure it would, but it wouldn't work for me. I thought Kip would love it if a woman talked dirty to him, whereas I'd feel awkward and more than a little doubtful that I could pull off what I lasciviously told Kip I'd do to him.

In spite of my nervousness, I decided to try it sometime down the road. Since we had just moved from Cleveland to Seattle, unpacking and settling in kept us busy, but an opportunity to exercise some dirty talking presented itself when Kip and I went downtown to the Seattle Science Center. There was a lecture going on about the evolution of planet Earth and the solar system. The first lecturer was great, but his buddy was convoluted and boring beyond belief. I told Kip I was leaving; he could stay and finish the lecture, I'd meet up with him later. Outside the Science Center, I went to a vendor for a scoop of Rocky Road in a sugar cone and walked the grounds, trying to kill time. I was so bored with everything that I guess my neurons finally rummaged through the attic to the very last thing they could find for me to play with: trying out naughty-thought thinking. I straightened my shoulders and walked back into the auditorium. I slid between the rows and sat down. Before I lost my nerve, I whispered in Kip's ear, "I want to suck you off."

He leaned away from me and gave me a quizzical look: "What?"

I leaned toward him and said, "When we get home I'm going to suck you until you get rock hard."

"Uh-huh," he replied in a surprisingly even tone.

I rubbed his thigh. "Then I'm going to get naked and take your cock slowly into me and slide up and down on it," I breathed.

He pursed his lips and seemingly nodded to himself like he knew what was happening. "It sounds good, but why are you telling me this right here?"

"Isn't it getting you hot? It's supposed to get you hot."

"Getting me hot is not my worry. Is it getting *you* hot?"

"It will . . . I mean, kinda, yes."

"Are those your 'naughty thoughts'? Are you experimenting with me, Joan?"

"Don't put it that way." I started to pout. "I should've never told you about that; now you're not surprised."

"Oh, jeez. I would've known something was up anyway. You don't talk like that."

"Well, just get used to it!" I said fiercely.

A couple of weeks later I got over my embarrassment at Kip's lack of response. To prevent a repeat of Kip's bemusement, I decided to prepare him for naughty words. So I told him: "Kip, there may be—no, there *are* going to be times where I'm going to say some salacious things outside the bedroom."

"You don't say salacious things *in* the bedroom."

"Ha ha. Do you want to help with this or what?"

"Whatever you say," he said, bending to examine a thread unraveling at the bottom of our curtains.

This was not going to be easy. The trick was to find a place or a situation where talking dirty would be an X-rated contrast to the event at hand. Something formal and boring is the best. Kip and I don't really do company functions or garden or cocktail parties or reunions. So I was limited to libraries, diners, coffee shops, and walks to the docks—oh, of course, and the supermarket and Staples. Okay, I'd work with what I had. Kip was prepared. And I had notes.

I made a few false starts, running a finger down his arm and then, "Kip . . ." But I chickened out. Finally, we decided to go to the supermall to find a jacket for me. Perfect. Lots of stores with lots of boring, frustrating waiting on Kip's part. A little hot and spicy from me should get a rise out of him (winky-wink). Sure enough, dragging him through all the stores with their tightly crammed carousels of clothes was getting audible sighs from him.

"Kip?"

"What?"

I tell him all the slithery, oily, nasty, slippery, suctiony things I will do to him. He asks, "Now? Good, let's get out of here." I tell him we can't go yet, I haven't found my jacket. This deflates him and I sense he isn't getting hot as much as looking for an excuse to get out of Banana Republic. Ticked off by his impassive mien, I wander around for another hour and a half. We go back home and I flop into a chair, exhausted, hoping he won't take me up on my prior proposal. Looking equally tired, he says he has a headache. A *headache*. Jeez.

Maybe there needed to be less time between my verbalizing my lust and doing something about it. Well, I'm not the type to have sex in wild places, otherwise known to me as *uncomfortable*. I tried again and again and we did have sex, but it seemed as if Kip was just trying to be obliging. Oh, sure, he was happy for the opportunity this afforded to have sex—especially at my behest. But somehow, I doubted it was the dirty talk that got him going. And did it ignite sexual passion in me? No, no, no. And really, wasn't it me that was supposed to be benefiting? In the back of my mind, I suspected this had turned into just another way to please my man.

The last time I gave public dirty talk a go, it was at Victoria's Secret. It was kind of a cheat because it was already a sexy place and I knew I might find a tingle there. We had gone again to the mall, and I dragged Kip to another clothing store as a diversion, then led him by the hand straight to Victoria's Secret. There we got to pick out va-va-voom thongs and corsets. I didn't have to say much, the lingerie did all the talking; from the look on his face, that's all he was listening to. My suspicions about the effect of dirty talk on Kip were soon confirmed. Right as I leaned toward his ear and started whispering something that would get his face burning, he actually shrugged by me and nearly sideswiped another woman in his effort to snap up some fishnets. Kip's murder during a Victoria's Secret sale. It's the only time I've seen him act like a linebacker at any sale at any clothing store. Now that's hot.

Twelve

POWER THONG

Maybe I needed to take naughtiness beyond just the verbal. I could think of doing risqué things. For example, I've read about going pantyless while shopping at the market. You needn't wear a dress so short that it's guaranteed to give someone a good look; you should wear one only short enough to make it *possible* for someone to get a good look. That's the danger. And it's deliciously naughty. I know I'm waiting for someone to up-skirt me.

I didn't own a dress that short. I also knew that I didn't have the gonads to do it. What if guys did see my rear end or pubes? Then they'd start dropping fruit and cans of Campbell's soup to get a peek. Then I'd get followed home by some guy who'd normally have me break into a run, waving my arms and screaming, "Call 911! Call 911!"

Plan two: go pantyless with my husband doing bodyguard duty as he gets off on the possibility that other men might catch a glimpse of the family jewels.

Too creepy.

All right, I'm not doing the no-panty thing. Thongs? It's a kind of compromise. Kip said he'd like me to wear thongs every day (under my pants) and that would be a turn-on for him—just knowing they were there. I could do that. We went to the women's department of Penney's and came to the thong section and Kip pointed to piles of underwear and said I should get three of that, get three of those, and five of that.

I did start wearing thongs, but I'm afraid only Kip gets sexy thoughts out of them. At first I thought, *This is cool. I am so hip.* As an added benefit, my tightest jeans slid on more easily. For a few weeks I imagined myself as a South American. *Tall and tan and young and lovely* . . . Nat King Cole croons.

But sometimes I long for my old cotton briefs. I like the breathable comfort. I like the fact that they don't ride the crack of my butt, which in my opinion is quite unhygienic unless you always have a pack of Wet Wipes handy. When Kip realized I was cheating on my own thongs with cotton undies, he was disappointed. So was I, especially when I read that thongs are empowering.

There is now something that can only be dubbed the *power thong*. One woman found thinking naughty-panty thoughts was just the thing to do in front of her boss. In an article in *O* magazine about empowering sex, the owner of Agent Provocateur said she received a fan letter from a woman working for the London Sunday Times who described "getting a chewing out from her boss, and she just let it roll over her." How did she manage that? She was "armored by the see-through red undies she was wearing under her pinstriped suit." It seems that just reminding yourself of your own sexiness can get you through some of the worst days the world or the workplace can dish out:

> *A lot of women want to feel good in a sexual way, too, and that's not necessarily about the act of sex. It's about delighting in your own curves, in your own body. Who would have thought that at my age, at 49, I'd be wearing a thong every day? No matter what's going on in the world, you can have this private party for yourself. You can go to work and know that underneath it all, you're hot.*

The thought of wearing lingerie to work so I can have a party in my pants would fill me with loathing if I imagined a *man* doing the same. I needed to meditate a few moments on that feeling. Why did the thought of a male coworker standing before me, pretending to listen to dull stories about the copier, but all the while giving himself pleasure at the thought of his own silly, naughtily tight underwear, make me shiver in disgust? Perhaps because I might think him incredibly emotionally and sexually immature, delighting in the "naughtiness" of wearing something frankly sexual, and getting off on the fact that unbeknownst to us, he is, tee-hee-hee, wearing it RIGHT HERE, in front of the boss and his coworkers, and they don't know it! Oh, goodness!

Most men, it seems, do not need to delight in their own bulges in order to feel sexual. They merely need to look at, or even imagine or recall, a pair of boobs or a pair of legs and it's boner time. But in magazine articles, women are always encouraged to think naughty, sexy thoughts. It's so cute when *we* do it. The more sexy the thoughts, the better, anytime, anywhere. Unfortunately, it appears that we suffer from a dearth of sexual thoughts about men, so we must rely on our own underwear.

But what is the point of wearing lingerie not known for its comfort or practicality underneath our work clothes? "Thongs, corsets, push-up bras—this is not a peep show for men," says *O* magazine, "it's a way women remind themselves of their playful, more erotic side." But I couldn't get over why a woman's erotic side always translates into the stuff of male fantasy instead of simply fantasizing about hard-bodied men and the sex we'll have with them.

One day I decided to really give the power-thong thing a good try. I thought I might have been too hasty in dismissing it. I don't particularly like the notion that women can up their sexual drive just by looking into the mirror at their own gorgeous selves. But in my heart, I believe that there may be some truth to it that I'm resisting. I mean, I've sort of felt it myself, but haven't given vanity its perhaps rightful role in my sexuality. Let's take the thong to a new level. After all, as fashion stands now, one of the points of wearing a thong is to be seen wearing a thong. The power comes from having the moxie to strut your stuff without caring if anyone thinks you're astonishingly brazen. Being sexually free is the whole point. So, if I was going to do it, I was going to do it right.

"Kip, maybe the thong would work if I put it . . . if we made it more . . . well, look here." I got out a long lace skirt with a slit up the side. There was no backing underneath the lace, just empty space. I put a black thong under it, and yep, you could easily see right through the skirt in any light. "I'll put on this skirt and the thong and you're going to take me to a club. How about that!" Kip gave me his bawdy British professor look. I returned it with Mae West gusto, bending my wrist upward and waving a pen around like one of those long cigarette holders.

We decided to go to The Mission, an upscale club just down the way. I got out my pink zirconium earrings, then put on a purple-red necklace shaped like some medieval weapon, then I painted my toenails magenta. This color scheme was chosen not so much out of preference but because of a hair-dye misadventure that left my hair a very bright burgundy. But, actually, tonight it looked good. I wore a low-cut lace belly shirt that went with the skirt and put a black bra underneath. No stockings. Black heels. Kip liked it a lot.

It was a two-and-a-half-block walk to The Mission. The temperature was in the forties and I grabbed a coat. Kip said, "Okay, if you want to, but this is about being out there in a thong. A coat? It's not going to do it for you." I agreed.

We walked out of the apartment and the chill hit me everywhere. The streets weren't crowded but there were smatterings of people chatting outside on cell phones or smoking. I felt very weird walking past them. I made no eye contact. Kip looked over at me and told me to straighten up. I had been hunching over—out of timidity, I guess. One thing I was certain of: I would not be able to walk down a street dressed like that if I didn't have Kip at my side.

So we're strolling down the street and this group of women starts to giggle just as I walk by. Okay, this is not good for the ego. I mean, hey, what the f——? I wanted to snatch the cell phones out of their hands and . . . wait . . . is that a *camera* phone? I'm very embarrassed now but that quickly turns to fury. "What is your problem, huh? Never seen an . . ." Kip grabs my elbow.

I turn to him, "Why didn't you do something?"

"What? What did you want me to do? Beat them up?"

"Yes."

I straightened my back and pulled back my shoulders. I walked proudly and with a little sway. I now felt defensive about my thonged butt and was daring anyone to titter or picture-phone it. I'd pop them in the chops. Meanwhile, Kip was looking from side to side, hoping the Harley-Davidson boys across the street in front of the Admiral Pub were not about to turn in our direction. Kip rarely wants to be put in the position of defending my honor, which that night appeared to be hiding between my butt cheeks. Personally, being wolf-whistled at is okay by me. However, the sight of tongues being thrust in and out between drunken lips would immediately disempower my thong. I wondered what we would do if those drunken Harley boys trotted across the street. Hopefully, I would have time to step out of my thong, grab that six-pack of Bud from the teenager at the corner, and launch the cans of beer from my thong like a slingshot—stopping the mob dead in its tracks.

I keep passing young women in front of the bars. I know they're making catty remarks. I feel a little deflated. Finally, we get to The Mission. It's jamming, it's loud, it's dark, and there's no place to walk and only a tiny table to sit at. I'm hoping to sit at the bar so everyone can get a nice look. The only one I see giving me a good look is a guy at the end of the bar. He kept glancing over at my backside. I kept stealing looks at him to make sure he was looking specifically at me. I wanted to get up and thank him. Then I wondered what he would have done if Kip (who was obliviously sucking on the ice in his Coke) hadn't been there. Buy me a drink? But then, would I want to get friendly with a guy who wanted to get friendly with the type of woman who would wear a transparent skirt and thong?

Kip was already bored and so was I. I was determined to get the last cherry out of my extra-tall glass of ginger ale, but couldn't stab at it through the ice.

"C'mon, Joan."

"I *want* that cherry." I never got it.

As we walked back, I asked Kip how he felt about my thong. "Nice." Did it get him hot?

"No, I didn't feel one way or the other about it. Except I got a little nervous about those guys hanging in front of the Admiral."

"So why does the thong work for you under my everyday jeans, but not in public?"

"I don't know if it works for me more, it's just kind of sexually satisfying to know that you have a woman that's a little racy day in and day out. You know?"

Once again, we walked those long blocks home. It was kind of a neat feeling, but not knowing what people were thinking kept it from being a supersexy adventure. I'd done it, but it hadn't made me feel powerful. It felt like a cheap thrill. Like streaking past an outdoor wedding.

"Hey, Kip?"

"Yeah."

"Did you see any guys looking at me?"

"Yeah, a couple of them at the bar."

I wonder what those guys were thinking? So easy to inflate and deflate me. Ah, the dubious sexual power of the thong. Hidden or revealed, it can make you feel the siren or it can make you feel unworthy to wear it. It giveth power and it taketh away.

It seemed anything and anyone had power over how sexy I felt, except me.

Thirteen

SWAPPING FANTASIES

As expected, I was not a naughty-thought natural, but I did have my share of sexual fantasies. I remembered Julie had asked if I felt safe enough to share my fantasies with Kip. In a word, no. But maybe if we swapped fantasies, we might be able to approximate them in our sexual encounters, and ergo, if I was living out my sexual fantasies, it might make me look forward to sex.

CONFRONTING THE DARK SIDE

The prospect of sharing my darkest fantasies, however, filled me with anxiety. I wanted to go through with it and get it over with, but I felt the walls begin to close in on me. It was better to get out of our apartment for this one.

I invited Kip out to Starbucks for a talk. I got my coffee and Kip got a Jones soda (one of his defects is that he's a non–coffee drinker). We sat at a table that was relatively far from the few other customers. I had brought a pen and notebook along in order to take notes. I wanted to write down exactly what fantasies we could live out and go over the logistics so that they would run as smoothly as possible.

"Okay," I said. "Let's get started. What's your sexual fantasy?"

"You already know mine," Kip replied.

Kip had free-floating fantasies. In terms of a woman's looks, he enjoyed a variety of women, most of them fitting the standard model types from men's magazines, soft-core porn, and other examples of pop culture. As for sex acts, besides intercourse and oral, he sometimes liked to be controlled, and sometimes he liked to take control. He was aroused by the image of a woman wearing leather or black vinyl lingerie with thigh-high boots—dominatrix gear—or maybe a sexy woman cop, and he fantasized about her taking charge. But he didn't have any desire to be whipped or spanked or put through other forms of pain. He just liked some light bondage accompanied by sensual sex acts of the more "vanilla" type. Other times, he would fantasize about putting a woman into some light bondage as he took on the role of the Gothic master of delight.

So what were my sexual fantasies? It was a little embarrassing. And it wasn't fair that I'd never fessed up before because Kip had been so honest with me about his.

I took a deep breath. I was starting to lose my nerve. Maybe this wasn't such a good idea after all. "Okay, all right. Jesus, this is tough. It's stupid. It's embarrassing . . ." Kip looked at me, waiting. I took a sip of my coffee, gulped. Then I looked at the bottom of my cup. "I need a refill." I procrastinate about everything, but it was especially dumb in this situation because where was I going to go? It wasn't like I had an escape plan or I wouldn't be seeing Kip again for a year. I had to volunteer something.

"You know," I said, "I used to have those kinds of fantasies, too." Kip looked at me some more. I really didn't want to go on. I already felt humiliated before saying a word. Hmm, am I having an emotional safety moment? Trust issues? Inhibitions that will force Kip out the door and I end up collecting glass unicorns into old age? I expelled a deep breath. "When I was an adolescent, I imagined these knights from the Middle Ages would ravish me." How stupid and immature. I was so embarrassed by this that I focused on my own feeling of being exposed rather than on Kip.

Kip asked, "So you were the damsel in distress having forced sex?"

"It was so long ago, I don't know—both damsel and prisoner, I guess, not really forced sex. Oh, I don't know, but something like that."

I was much better at facing his fantasies than mine. The strange thing was that I told him about a fantasy I had when I was a teenager rather than any I had now. It seemed like an appropriate fantasy for a teen girl who thought of the Knights of the Round Table. That fantasy was long gone, but because it was embarrassing anyway, it appeared I was breaking down and revealing something intimate about myself. In reality, it was a smoke screen, a way I could save face by pretending I had outgrown all that stuff years ago. I had matured. Of course, this put Kip in the position of being the one who had *not* matured. He had such baroque fantasies. Mind you, I didn't inwardly feel that way, but it just showed how willing I was to let Kip twist in the wind and be vulnerable and maybe feel a little embarrassed, too, while I stayed cloaked as an example of refined, higher-brained development.

But he caught me. "You know, you didn't tell me about your fantasies now. Current fantasies. Why? Don't you have any?" he asked.

Now this was a sticky wicket. If I told him I had no fantasies, then I must be a sexless freak. If I did tell him my fantasies, I'd take myself back to possible humiliation. And adding to this bad stew, if I admitted I had fantasies, I might have to act them out instead of masturbating to them. That was the whole point of our little talk, but I was having second thoughts about making my fantasies real. And that I would rather be my own uninhibited, wild, passionate lover might seem just a jot unfair to my sex-deprived husband.

"Current fantasies? Like now?" I wasn't exactly sure what the phrase "being deliberately obtuse" meant, but I was pretty sure it applied to me.

"Yes, *now*. What did you think I meant?"

"Okay," I said, expelling another big breath. "I'm out of the knight thing. I'm not, like, into . . . I don't what you'd call it really. But I have this recurring fantasy . . . God, this is . . . man, I *hate* talking about this stuff!" Then I remembered how tough it had been for Kip and how brave he had been to tell me about his fantasies. It had to be a two-way street. "All right, here it is: I'm in this cruddy apartment building that has this great-looking landlord. Except he's a real pig—I can't pay the rent he wants, so then he says he won't evict me if I work the rent off by having sex with him. And so, I hate his guts, but—what's a girl to do?" I said, widening my eyes and putting a finger to my dimple. I started nervously laughing, then sat back in my chair to signal it was all out in the open now, and didn't I feel that was a weight off!

"Huh," Kip said thoughtfully.

"Yeah, I don't know what kind of thing that was, it wasn't forced sex, per se . . ."

"Coerced sex," Kip volunteered.

"Yeah, blackmail. And because he keeps raising the rent and adding fees, well, I never can catch up. And if I run off without paying him, he tells me he'll have me arrested for cheating him out of his money and I'll be sent to debtor's prison."

"There is no debtor's prison anymore," he pointed out.

"Yeah, I know. Never mind. I threw a little Dickens in there."

"So, how does it work? He just comes over and demands you give him sex?"

"Yeah, he reminds me I owe him, then we're suddenly naked and he pins me down, we do it, then he gloats and leaves."

"Actually, I have some fantasies about taking an unwilling woman, too," Kip admitted. "Of course, she always ends up enjoying it and eggs me on."

"Right, that's pretty much like mine. At first I'm repelled or afraid, but after a while I lose control and start moaning and really loving it—that's the part that's really against my will because it means he broke through my—I don't know—my determination not to enjoy sex with him."

"Exactly!" Kip said, sounding relieved that we weren't so at odds. "Yeah, and really, I can go both ways. I like being overwhelmed by a forceful, sexy woman, but I also like taking control during sex."

"Huh, I don't think I've had a dominatrix-type fantasy."

"No, it doesn't have to be about flogging or stuff like that. It's more attitude than anything else. But let's just leave that aside for now. Let's start by concentrating on your primary fantasy first. If that gets you going and you're happy, I guarantee I'll be happy, too."

DIRTY PICTURES AND BLACKMAIL

This was Kip's plan to replicate my fantasy: he couldn't blackmail me with eviction, but he could blackmail me with compromising pictures of my glorious self. Hmm. Okay, that might work. But already I was getting leery about the whole thing. I had seen an episode of *Judge Judy* a couple of weeks before, where a woman was suing her ex-boyfriend for the return of some naked, lewd photos. Judge Judy looked down at the weeping woman and said, "Ugh, that is just plain dumb. Do you know how many times I've heard this?"

But that was just a boyfriend. This was my husband. It's what a lot of couples do. It's even encouraged by some sexperts so that your spouse will fantasize to *your* pictures. On the other hand, our marriage wasn't doing all that well. That sort of put me into possible ex territory. Then again, what would Kip do with them anyway? Get them made into playing cards? Sell them on eBay, where the chief embarrassment would be that the lowest bidder turned out to the highest bidder?

All right, let's do it.

I noticed that Kip was having a pretty good time posing me. Very *Playboy*. The compromising pictures were done. Then Kip took the camera and said he was going to hide the pictures where I wouldn't be able to find them. After that, he would initiate sex by reminding me of the photos and demanding his due.

First I had to get over the sheer awkwardness of the whole venture; that's especially hard when you're enacting your own fantasies. It was difficult because we didn't have a screenplay to go by. But Kip improvised and he actually did a good job of it. His aggressive initiation of sex was pretty good the first time, but I didn't have an orgasm, and despite the erotic charge I felt from it, I didn't have an eager desire to go again. And the results only became more mediocre on subsequent tries. This favorite fantasy that had served so well for the past year or so deteriorated in sexual intensity once I acted it out. It was like a hurricane hitting land, breaking up and slowing down. After a few times I told Kip it wasn't doing it for me.

Kip said he really didn't care much if we acted out his fantasy at all, he just wanted more sex period. Vanilla was fine by him. He said he enjoyed it all. He didn't care about his own fantasies, he had wanted to put more emphasis on mine.

Kip bought some of those fur-lined cuffs to up the ante for me (and using the cuffs also played nicely into his own fantasies about taking control). But it still didn't do it for me. He asked what he could do differently, what I wanted or needed. But what could I say? The prologue made me antsy. I still got anxious during sex because, like Pamela, I only felt a pang of lust during the last two minutes before I'd come—*if* I'd come. And sometimes I know I'm not going to come, end of story. I don't want to reenact the children's book *The Little Engine That Could*, puffing up a mountain, saying, "I think I can, I think I can, I think I can." They say the brain is the most important sexual organ. It starts in your head first. But that's stretching it. Most things start in the head first. Well, I'd like it to reflect in my loins.

After a while we let it go. I simply wasn't into that fantasy anymore—maybe because I didn't want to spend a half hour or more enacting it with another human. That's a sad fact. I didn't want to spend a half hour having sex, and it seemed that no kind of fantasy, even my own, even when carefully orchestrated, could overcome my impatience with the sex act.

Naturally, Kip was disappointed. Our role play was over. Fortunately, it turns out Kip had destroyed the naked photos of me just after he took them—that's why I'd "never be able to find them." But now what? Hell, how could I get more desire to be game even for vanilla sex, period?

Fourteen

SENSATE FOCUSING

If the sensual-awareness school was right, my problem was my failure to focus on the sensation of sex. I needed to become more aware of the feel of his skin on mine, the moist softness of his lips as they caressed different parts of my body, to focus on his fingers brushing up against my thighs, the feel of his chest. I should inhale his musky aroma. Then, finally, focus on the exquisite sensation of fullness and friction as he pressed his turgid manhood into the welcoming lotus of my womanhood.

After reading such advice, I rubbed my hands quickly up and down together, took a deep breath, and let it out with a whoosh! Then I let my arms drop to my side and shook them out. This is my way of prepping myself for a big task at hand. I was a pole-vaulter before the vault, the marathoner before the marathon, the discus thrower before the throw.

This was going to be the ultimate challenge because focusing is something that's very hard for me. And I took this challenge seriously because I thought it had a good chance of working. I agreed with the premise that I was too worried about Kip and about performing—sounded right. And yet I was still haunted by a transpersonal psychology class I had taken in college. My professor, Dr. Sollod, thought that meditation and mandalas were the secret to peace of mind, being centered and all the other spiritual stuff I wanted. But when he gave us focus exercises to do, I failed them miserably. He'd say, just start out meditating just a minute and then increase your time from there. I started out with a minute and *de*creased from there.

But, why not? So one Saturday I decided to give sensate focusing a try. I went to the health-food store and got some scented body oils and new incense I hoped wouldn't be overpowering. Then, while Kip was busy on the computer, I went into the bedroom and got it nice and perfumed up. I put on some come-hither outfit and sauntered into the living room. When I came up behind him, he spun around and gave me a whistle. Ooh la la. I said, "C'mon, big boy," or something clichéd like that. It's that humor-defense-mechanism thing again. I can't just play it straight, I have to come out like Lauren Bacall, leaning melodramatically against a door frame. I told Kip I was ready for a little sensual fun and took his hand and led him toward the bedroom. He took in the ambience of the candles and then turned to me and said, "Nice."

Then, maybe a little overanxious about pleasing me, he said he had to get ready himself. He disappeared into the bathroom and I heard water running in the sink. Minutes passed. I went to the door and said, in what I hoped was a light voice, "Hey, whatcha doing in there?"

"Shaving!"

"Okay, don't take too long," I said in a singsong voice.

More time went by. I looked around to see if there was anything else to prepare. Nope. So I sat down and turned on the television. Then I heard the shower. Jesus! I went and snuffed out one of the candles, because it was on the verge of drowning itself, and then the incense, so it wouldn't stink to high heaven by the time he got out. I was a little annoyed, but I couldn't fault Kip. I liked to shower and shave before sex myself. But I was struggling to keep my head in a relaxed yet very focused mental state. I plopped back down on the sofa and put my stilettoed feet up on the coffee table. And waited.

It probably wasn't all that long before Kip got out of the shower (eighteen minutes, not including the shaving time, but who's counting!), but because my preparatory state of relaxed focus hung in a delicate balance, it seemed like forever. The shower stopped, so I swung my legs off the coffee table, leaped to my feet, and tottered into the bedroom. I grabbed the lighter and relit the candles, got the incense going, and then I checked myself in a hand mirror. I took a breath and looked at my reflection. *Center yourself. Relax. Focus. Enjoy.*

Kip came out of the shower in his best pajama bottoms. He looked wonderful. In spite of this, I felt a tingle of nerves. I mentally shook it off, letting my eyes linger over his body. I took him by the hand and led him into the bedroom. I told him to sit on the bed. He looked up at me and smiled. I put on some music with a deep, sensual beat. I told him to lie down. He complied. I took the scented oil from the dresser and put a good amount into my cupped hand. I let it warm there for a minute, making myself aware of its liquidity, then I massaged the hand-warmed oil into his chest. I focused on the feel of the liquidity of the oil against the rough hair of his chest. A beautiful contrast of textures, I told myself. Hey, I'm not too bad at this.

I told him to turn over and oiled his back (so smooth!), and then his legs (swimmer's thighs!), and then I centered mischievously around his buttocks (naughty and luscious), and then tantalizingly onto his testicles (aww, he trimmed the pubic hair on them—so considerate!). I focused on all his swoops and curves and the way my fingers played along them.

Was any of this heightening my desire? Sure. I mean it had to be. I was definitely more sensually aware, more sensually aware of Kip's body. Okay, so it wasn't exactly making me hot. Was feeling sensual the same as sensual feeling? Let's not dwell.

I handed the oil to Kip and said, "Now it's my turn." I was still wearing my lingerie, which consisted of a white bustier, thong, and fishnets. In a way, I was disappointed that I'd have to take it all off to get the oil job. I had put a lot of effort into putting it on. But maybe we could make a sexy game of it. I had Kip unhook my bustier. It wasn't an easy job. He really couldn't get the hang and pretty soon he was frowning with concentration. My first inclination was to jump in and help. But that would've meant pushing worrying about Kip to the forefront. I wasn't going to do that anymore. And I wanted to show Kip that I was perfectly confident that he knew his way around a woman's lingerie. So I arched my back and turned my head to the side as if I was getting off on how his fingers slowly but insistently sought to reveal my magnificent breasts.

After revealing those two beauties, Kip wiped the sweat from his brow. I convinced myself the sweat was the physical manifestation of his passion. I saucily puckered my lips at him and then languorously laid myself back upon my Martha Stewart pillows.

He knelt on the bed beside me and poured some oil into his

own hands. He massaged the oil into my breasts. It felt good. It really did. I closed my eyes and let the sensation roll over me. "Mmmmm. That . . . that's so nice," I murmured. "Stay right there." He did. But eventually he moved down, to my ribs, and then slowly to my thighs. I couldn't help it, I opened one eye, lifted my head the teeniest bit off the pillow, and saw that Kip had a boner. It was kind of funny-looking because he was kneeling, and he looked like some kind of souvenir fertility god. And then I thought to myself, *Joan, you are not supposed to be thinking this crap. Your mind is wandering. Bring it back!* I lay back down, kept my eyes closed, and promised myself that I'd concentrate only on the sensual.

Kip stopped and I felt him shifting on the bed. Probably pouring more oil into his hand. Yup, I was right. He began to massage the inside of my thighs again. Suddenly I found myself becoming anxious again. And I was becoming anxious because instead of getting more and more *into* it, I was getting more and more out of it. Maybe we needed to move on. Instead of feeling the pleasure, I got up on my elbows and said in a sexy voice, "Boy, that was great."

It certainly isn't the case that Kip's not a sensitive lover. Kip knows what makes women tick sexually. Indeed, he pays homage to my clit. As well he should. It's a hot button. I've pressed it not a few times myself to get that quick, reliable orgasm. And there he is down there, licking my thighs, kissing my breasts, and giving me proficient, thorough tongue—again, not my thing, but maybe I could just get used to it. Again, there were times I'd have a twinge here and there, and sometimes I would come, but even then I just wanted him to get it *over* with.

I knew I was supposed to love getting good head and long foreplay. I knew to even demand it. But as the weeks dragged on, and the sexual episodes dragged on, I felt like I was trapped in a crowded subway car. Suddenly I wanted him to just hurry up. I didn't care about having an orgasm—just get off of me. I couldn't breathe for the closeness. Just as I was ready to twist his head off of his neck, he looked up at me and smiled, checking to see if I was having a good time. Damn.

Sensate focusing helped to a point. But it was still work. I still had to think my way through sex. It would be so much easier if I had a man's robust desire for sex. Instead of focusing on my most fleeting thoughts of sex with the concentration of a Vulcan mind-meld, it would be great if I was just so damn horny, just looking at my husband glistening after a shower made me want to leap across the bed and grab him like he was the last doughnut in the break room.

Fifteen

SPIRITUAL SEX

*P*ut it in perspective. That's the key. Sex need not be just an animal urge. Sex is increasingly being equated with spirituality. I found that out while I was waiting on a prescription at the drugstore.

I had a good fifteen to twenty minutes to browse. I didn't mind because I could catch up on some of my reading at the magazine racks: *Time, Newsweek, Cat Fancy, Muscle, Maxim, FHM.* (I couldn't believe Barbara Walters would pose like that on the cover!) And Oprah, looking fabulous, was touting a spiritual issue of *O* magazine. After living on the edge of hysteria and angst all my life, inner peace and a wise outlook was something I craved. Could the answers I sought be craftily hidden in a talk-show host's magazine? I pulled down the magazine, leaned against the rack, and began thumbing through it. Lovely pictures of pastoral scenery (sometimes marred by positive affirmations written across the bottom), various articles on finding oneself by losing oneself to the world, rituals, sacred spaces, pants that will minimize the size of your ass, and how to learn spiritual lessons from the universe.

Then the clincher that made me plunk down four bucks: "Spiritual Sex." *O* magazine was coming home with me. I needed to think of sex as a spiritual connection, said the article. Having always felt that I could use some spirituality to center myself, I willed myself to keep an open mind and be persuaded that I could get in touch with this inner quality through sex. Sex certainly wouldn't have been my preferred method of becoming more Buddha-like, but whatever gets me there is good. I'd kill two birds with one stone. The more I thought about it, the more I liked the idea.

ALL THINGS SENSUAL

I left the drugstore and turned right toward the new deli. The coffee came from standing carafes, and if you don't hit them at just the right time they will dump out bitter, lukewarm coffee. I put my cup under the spout and turned it on. No steam.

At home, the coffee was comfortably heating in the microwave as I leaned on my elbows reading the *O* magazine: "When sex takes on a spiritual dimension, there's a sense of oneness with yourself, your partner and the universe," says Ogden, a sex therapist and sex researcher. "There's a heightened sensuality and a feeling of transcendence."

And once you've locked into that, the article said, you can connect with all sorts of lovely, sensual experiences you never would have noticed before.

To start, I needed to become more sensually aware of my surroundings: the feel of a breeze caressing my skin, the moistness of the grass under bare feet, the lushness of a peach. This sounded like a good practice. I'm seldom aware of my surroundings; instead I'm listening to the constant grumbling in my own head. Why not replace it with something beautiful? I needed to stop and smell the roses. Well, I did do that at the market. And I enjoyed it, but the rest of the day I'd be shut off to everything else. I was just one big, angry brain moving through the city.

So, let's start with my body. Wear something flowy. I looked in the closet and there's nothing flowy. Okay, forget flowy. Get a peach. I can easily get sensual around food. A great excuse to purchase something expensively out of season. I'll take a little trip to the market—not Safeway, the expensive one.

The day was a little cool, so I went to get my coat, then I thought *No, experience the weather, don't hide from it.* I congratulated myself for the thought and went out with nothing but a T-shirt. My skin got goose pimples and I felt the coolness on my skin, my neck, and my sockless feet. At the market I took in the baskets of fruit, all artfully arranged. I grabbed some grapes. They were a thousand bucks a pound, but what the hell. Then I got a mango, a peach, and a half-pint of golden raspberries from an organic farm run by Trappist monks in Equatorial New Guinea. Such wild, exotic colors and flavors to savor. I passed by the bakery and there was an éclair staring me right in the face. It would've been criminal to pass this chance at a sensual, spiritual communion. I've had oral sex with éclairs before, so I knew this would be a reliably sumptuous experience.

I started eating the peach the minute I got out of the store. The juices started running down my chin, a sensual experience to be sure, but kind of a bad one. I was all drippy and my wet chin was uncomfortably cold in the same wind that had so refreshingly caressed me just minutes before. I wiped my face with the heel of my hand. I was disappointed with myself for not enjoying this excursion into sensuality more. But it had only been my first day, so I shouldn't have expected instant results—it's a mind-set, a lifestyle, and one that can't be had in a few days. And . . . how could I forget? I looked fondly at the white paper bag. My beautiful, beautiful éclair.

Having successful sensuous experiences with chocolate, I decided to use it as a sex toy. (But what had this to do with spirituality?) My husband was not into food as a sex enhancer, but he did it for me. We tried the old whipped-cream thing and it was awful. It liquefied moments after it contacted skin and slid off either side of his body. We tried honey. Again, not successful. But that was some time ago and this time I thought we'd cut the crap and get to what I really wanted: chocolate. You could put chocolate on a tire and I'd lick it off.

I later took Kip to the store and we tried to figure out what might work. Hot fudge sauce? Love it, but too hard to spread. Frosting? Of course! We went to the bakery aisle and I got dark and milk-chocolate frosting in those peel-back cans. I hadn't eaten frosting out of a can since I was a teenager. But now I had full permission. Would this be sensual? Oh, you bet, baby!

Friday night rolled around and I was actually looking forward to sex. After eating moderately healthy all week, I was waiting to unleash an all-you-can-lick-up frosting session. My husband, who would just happen to be under the frosting, would equally benefit (not to mention providing some interesting terrain for my chocolate landscape). He showered, got naked, and lay flat on his back. I got out the can of frosting and knelt by the bed, wondering where I should apply it first. In order for this to be a more sensual and spiritual experience, I had learned not to go for the genitals first. I'd start at the thighs, then the chest, and so on. I started by applying some frosting gently to a thigh, then licking it off. Then to the other thigh, and slowly licking that off. Ooh, yeah, I must be giving him shivers.

The only bad thing was—no not bad, but perhaps a wee bit of a downside—the mounting heat of the chocolate. It didn't slide off like the whipped cream, but his body heat, well, it made it warm and a little melty and the trouble is I do not like warm chocolate. Finally, I got to the portion of the show where he was to become my chocolate lollipop. I laid the frosting on real thick and quickly attacked (less time for the chocolate to become heated through). It went pretty well. I got my chocolate fix, he got great lubrication, and—how shall I put it politely?—suction. There was an indelicate incident in which a pubic hair got into the mix. There was no way to extricate it because it was mixed in with a glob of frosting. But none of this was fatal to the experiment.

What was fatal was going to the bathroom afterward and seeing to my shock that my face had chocolate all over it. And not in a cute way, where you see a darling little smudge on the forehead, the tip of one's nose, or the chin. No, it was a huge chocolate ring around my mouth that, for some odd reason, left my lips bare. I looked like Al Jolson in one of those horrid twenties black minstrel shows. Did Kip let me go on like that? Did he notice? I ran back into the bedroom and said, "Look at me!" in exasperation. He looked up and laughed. I went back out and pouted. I put the remaining frosting into the refrigerator. The next morning, I ate the rest of it for breakfast (downside number two).

The next night Kip asked how I liked the sex. "Well," I said, reaching for a slice of pizza, "I didn't like the frosting smeared all over my face. What about you, did that bother you?"

"I didn't really notice until you showed me. That was pretty funny, Joan."

"I looked ridiculous."

"The only thing I didn't really like was all the licking. I'm not into that much licking."

"What? Licking of where?" Man, now he tells me!

"It's . . . licking my legs and chest and neck, it just doesn't do anything for me. So you don't have to do that anymore. Now the oral sex—that was great."

"Okay, but it's so messy."

"So what? If you like it, who cares?"

We tried it two more times. But though frosting is delicious for oral sex, it didn't do a darn thing for the rest of sex.

Screw it. I felt kind of bad that I had to be lured toward sex by chocolate anyway. I was taking the easy way out instead of changing my mind-set. Frosting was not a spiritual connection. It wasn't what *O* magazine meant by opening up your senses. "Our sexuality isn't separate from the rest of us; it's an integral part of ourselves. It can't be cordoned off and ignored or negated if we want to feel complete. It's another avenue for integrating body, mind, and spirit—ultimately another step on our path to wholeness.

How in the world can I get there from here? That's huge. Go back to the drawing board. The problem is I do feel complete without sex, it's my husband who's left wanting.

Sixteen

MAKING LOVE

The Better Sex Video Series promised to be "the most enjoyable, comfortable way you and your partner can learn in the privacy of your own home." I saw this line of videos on a shelf at a lovers' boutique called Ambiance. According to the box covers, the videos were narrated by several doctors or psychologists and featured real, caring, loving couples learning how to better their relationships.

While Kip was staring in horror at the world's biggest dildo, I sidled up and showed him the video. He turned the video box over, reading the back. He wasn't impressed.

"Are you sure you want this?" he asked.

"Yeah, why not," I said resignedly. "I know, it's probably crap. But it's got doctors and therapists. And it says it's got real couples learning how sex gets them back to being loving couples. So it's not like porn."

When we got home, Kip asked if I wanted to watch it alone or with him. I wanted to say alone. I didn't want to watch it with him because I might not like the suggestions, or how easily everything was resolved on the video. And if Kip liked it, I might be stuck countering his enthusiastic response. But that was foolish. "C'mon, sit down next to me."

"Do you want me to make some popcorn?"

I looked at him, "Are you serious?"

"Sort of."

We watched "Volume 1: Better Sexual Techniques." I'd say it was good if you didn't know your way around sex too well, but other than that, nah. The stories were clichéd, and I couldn't help but focus on the physical looks of the couples. Robert never took the time to give his wife pleasure, and she thought all she could expect was the old wham-bam. Then they got wise to the ways of foreplay, namely, cunnilingus.

I leaned over to Kip. "Doesn't Robert look like Alan Thicke from *Growing Pains*?"

"Yeah, yeah, he does!"

"It's the hair, too. That thick woolly, hair. I can't tell where his head leaves off and her muff begins."

We had to fast-forward through the sound of Robert's constant munching and munching—over the background score of tinkling pianos, no less.

Kip got up. "God, he looks like a mad badger down there."

"Where are you going?"

"I'm getting some potato chips."

"Do you want me to put it on pause?"

"No, please don't."

Then there was Bill and Virginia (whom Kip missed). Bill showed up at Virginia's place of work. Luckily, she wasn't in a gray cubicle. No, she had a huge office and a big desk for him to hide under while he ate her out. Then the secretary walked in, but didn't see him. That put a smile on his wet face.

Then we got to the real spiritual part of our program. The last couple, Donna and Gary, had some serious problems with their marriage because of sex—no, *lovemaking*. The score in the background was the tranquil type you hear on a wildlife segment where the camera captures a flower opening, pans over a meadow, and shows us the birds and bunnies that live there to indicate how beautiful and sweet this all is; an expression of the deepest love, intimacy, and commitment. There's even a gentle voice-over from Donna, narrating how strong and intimate their marriage has become: "Now that our sex life has been transformed, our entire marriage has become healthier, happier; we're stronger . . . and we're more aware of each other." I thought it was just a wee bit disconcerting because during the pastoral music and the gentle voice-over, what the viewer sees is Donna on her back, her legs way up in the air, and Gary's testicles slapping against her buttocks. Cue more meadow music.

Kip had an expression on his face that looked like he just swallowed the worm at the bottom of a tequila bottle. "Good grief! That wasn't pretty."

After the sex segment, Gary was interviewed. He was choking up a little and on the verge of tears as he recounted how learning Better Sex saved his marriage: "Our relationship means more to me than anything in my life. And it means enough to me to do whatever it takes to see it grow and be nurtured." I'm sure Gary was willing to do whatever it took—however much sex it might take, however many positions they had to try—will this man never stop suffering for love? I put one hand over my heart while wiping tears from my eyes with the other. Someone, please, provide me with some delicately scented tissue.

AH, IT'S SPIRITUAL FOR *HIM*

The sensual and spiritual schools were not successful in getting me into that transcendent, sacred view of sex I thought would result from being aligned with the universe. This was grievously disappointing. My libido remained flat. What I was about to find out was that it wasn't me that needed to be spiritually fulfilled through sex; it was my husband.

Dr. Pat Love helps us get into the spirit by giving several examples of how men feel when their wives are less than enthusiastic about sex. According to Dr. Love, the men say they feel frustrated, emotionally bottled up, and rejected when they don't get sex. They described themselves as feeling castrated, humiliated, angry, irritated, worthless, and even embarrassed. Love recounts the tale of a couple in their thirties who've had a "five-year stalemate" regarding sexual frequency. Both took turns describing their own sexuality. Love reports that Karen was surprised to learn how important sex was to Arnold:

> *What touched Karen most was hearing Arnold describe how he felt when he had gone without sex for several days. It was so different from her experience. From her point of view a week without sex was a vacation. It allowed her to catch up on her sleep and do more reading. She joked to Arnold that her "reading drive" was stronger than her sex drive.*

As you know, I myself doubt that last sentence was a joke.

When Arnold describes the emotional pain he feels from a lack of sex, and how his "psyche grows harder and smaller" and how isolated it makes him feel, not just from his wife, "but from everyone around me," Karen gets a case of the guilts. Karen had previously thought that sex for Arnold was just like an itch that needed to be scratched. Now she knows that depriving her husband of sex has a global effect on his psyche and even his spiritual connectedness in life. John Gray agrees; a man's sexual satisfaction is conducive to his flourishing spirituality and connectedness to beauty, life, and love: "A man's persistent sexual longing is really his soul seeking wholeness. The barren landscape of living only in his mind seeks union with the rich, sensuous, colorful, sweet-smelling terrain of his heart."

Try saying no to that. You'd be such a bitch.

So what's a girl to do? Perhaps I was doing things backward. Perhaps it wasn't me who was prone to having a spiritual awakening through sex, it was men. Kip wasn't just chasing his animal desires. He was releasing the very part of him from which love flowed, so to speak. I had to recognize that sex for men was massively different from sex for women. It was a soul thing. The part of themselves that opened up their love, their emotions, and their vulnerability toward their significant other. Sex was the zipper to their heart.

MAKING LOVE

Except, I wasn't convinced that sex is primarily, or even usually, an expression of love. Who hasn't seen many times over in human sexual behavior that love and sex need not coexist?

I think "making love" was a term that started out as a polite euphemism for having sex and is now taken literally. The term went out of style for a while in the sixties and seventies when how-to sex books favored a more straightforward rendering of sexuality that needed no euphemisms to validate it. Now it is difficult to find self-help books (usually targeted to women) that don't use the term "making love" ad nauseam.

I doubt the reasoning behind the present use of this euphemism is to save our tender ears from explicit mention of the deed. Not at all. It is to convince women that what they are doing each and every time they have sex with their boyfriend or husband is a loving thing for him. And it was beginning to seem to me that "making love" is a term the experts most especially reserve for those times when we may need to have unwanted sex with our husbands.

But surely it is also true that for men sexual excitement often occurs at the thought of a one-night stand with a stranger. Many men view Internet sites advertising "sluts" who just ask to be screwed instead of made love to. And indeed, men do pay sex workers and the porn industry lots of money for the privilege of not "making love." Hugh Hefner, that silken-robed scalawag, did not have honeymoon suites at the Playboy Mansion.

But *women* are told that sex is the most profound form of intimacy in a marriage. The sexperts would have us assume that after they get into a committed relationship, sex undergoes a magical transformation in men's minds, from a drive that causes them to pant after women in bars and nightclubs looking to get laid, into a beautiful expression of emotional regard. But if men did think of sex as love, we wouldn't have to worry about men getting bored sexually in a marriage. Can a man get tired expressing his love for his dear wife? Even if that is possible, why would the sexperts recommend adding a little kink to the proceedings? Would doing it doggy style with his wife in a plaid skirt revitalize their spiritual connection?

Has being married meant that sex has become a spiritual communion with my beloved and the deepest expression of love? Sometimes. But if you're having sex on a regular basis, you are not going to be doing it each time out of love. Philosopher Simone de Beauvoir, a gutsy woman, said that marital sex can become merely "joint masturbation." The wife may imagine she's being forcefully taken, "that her husband is not himself but an *other*." The same holds true for him: "The husband enjoys the same dream; in his wife he is possessing the legs of some dancer he has seen on the stage, the bosom of a pin-up girl whose picture he has looked at, a memory, an image." Or the husband needs to become a voyeur to become excited, "to feel again a little of the old magic." If it benefits sex in the marriage, sexperts encourage husbands and wives to mentally substitute other people for their spouse as long as the aim is to keep the sex—er, *intimacy*, hot.

Philosopher Richard Taylor gets down to brass tacks:

> *If you try to divest the thing of its passional associations— so as to be blinded as little as possible—and bring clearly before your mind an actual image of the culmination and goal of the erotic drive [the sex act], you can see that nothing could possibly be more totally absurd, nothing less likely as a candidate for a sane being's aspiration.*

As a kid, I thought the same thing. Having no sexual desire yet, I looked at sex with neutral vision, one might say. And it seemed unimaginable. Only real lust makes such an act seem perfectly desirable.

Perhaps this is why women are more likely than men to feel that sex can be repulsive even within a marriage, even when they know that sex is sanctioned by church and state—because we are less blinded by lust. Unless a woman is feeling just as lustful as a man when engaging in sex, sex will seem embarrassing, shameful, and yes, even dirty.

Joanna, a newlywed, said that sometimes sex made her feel dirty. But Dr. Phil told her, "It's clean, it's wholesome, it's natural and it is OK to have fun. . . . It's OK to enjoy that. And you've got to give yourself that permission." Well, sex may be natural, but that doesn't make it clean, wholesome, good fun. That's a day playing badminton at the park. Since Joanna complains she feels dirtiest when her husband, Chad, attempts "something different," it's probably not because he's looking for an even more wholesome experience with his wife. Sex isn't any more wholesome simply because Joanna and Chad are having it within holy matrimony.

Woody Allen's answer to the question of whether sex is dirty was "Only if it's done right." Men (and more than a few women) don't prefer wholesome sex; they want a dirty good time. That leaves women not knowing where the line should be drawn. A woman once wrote to columnist and sex pundit Dan Savage asking why some men enjoy ejaculating onto the faces of their sex partners:

> *I am a female in a relationship with a male. Through him I have, of course, become aware of the prevalence in straight male pornography of coming on women's faces . . . No one has ever come on my face, but if someone did, I know I would feel pretty degraded. So tell me, Dan, why does something so degrading to the other person figure in these fantasies?*

Savage responded:

> *Coming all over someone's face doesn't just* seem
> *degrading, YECCH, it actually is degrading, and it's precisely*
> *that reason so many people get off on it. Coming on*
> *someone's face is not about sweet, sweet love; it's about hot,*
> *hot sex. There is a "marking my territory" element to it, and*
> *I'm happy to report that it's a kind of symbolic violation of the*
> *person whose face is being ejaculated on. As the man comes,*
> *he's thinking, "Oh, yeah, she wants my dick so f——kin' bad*
> *that she'll let me shoot all over her f——king face."*

It is this "sexy, degrading, erotic charge," Savage noted, "that in-
spires some men to come all over women's faces."

As Taylor said of sex:

> *Clearly, it is no form of love at all, beyond the fact that it*
> *happens to be called by that name . . . Love, as a sentiment,*
> *expresses itself naturally in sympathetic kindness, even*
> *sometimes in a kind of identification of oneself with the*
> *thought, feelings, and aspirations of another. It is compatible*
> *with sexual passion, but it by no means rests on it nor,*
> *contrary to what so many would like to believe, does it find its*
> *highest expression there.*

Of course, that's not to say that men and women can't enjoy a
sentimental communion while having sex. I just wonder if much of
this emphasis on nurturing and spiritual closeness is to feminize
sex for our protection. A way for women to deliver sex from the car-
nal into the realm of the spiritual.

OH, IT'S ABOUT MENTAL DESIRE FOR *HER*

And we may need deliverance at times. Dr. Love, bless her, does come right out and say that in general, women have a lower sex drive than men and there's little we can do about that biological fact:

> *Although society's view of sexuality may change, there appears to be an underlying biological constant. Studies of human cultures around the world have shown that most men think about sex more often, are more easily aroused, want sex more frequently, desire more partners, and masturbate more often than most women.*

Finally, I thought as I read this passage, someone who has showed her cards. Someone who stated what I thought was obvious. Men wanted sex more than women. I am not crazy. It's true!

But even while acknowledging substantial differences in desire between the sexes, even assenting to it having a biological basis, Love seems to wave away the intractability of the differences. According to her, there is biological desire, and then there is "mental desire." And if you (women) don't have enough of the former, you could probably substitute the latter. Of course, this perked up my ears. I'm vain enough to think that through sheer brainpower and lofty sentiments, I can, with proper effort, focus, and loving compassion, think my way into a sexually charitable spirit. All I needed to do was create in myself mental desire. A woman's motivation for this mental desire, say sexperts like Love and Gray, is to give the gift of spiritual sex to her man. Dr. Love believes that by thinking of sex as a loving *gift* to our men, women can avoid the resentment that they may feel having undesired sex.

> *Celebrate your mental desire. You can be a wonderful sex partner even if you have low sexual desire. Your willingness to satisfy your partner's needs and to create more sexual desire in yourself is a cause for celebration. Rejoice in your positive attitude and be assured that the two of you can create a long-lasting, mutually satisfying sexual relationship.*

Hearing Love's bubbly, pep-rally tone gives me cause for concern. I can smell false notes of enthusiasm in it. I know her heart is in the right place. She just wants couples to get along. But thinking of sex as a gift is a trick of mind that could get old after a while. I've done my share, and so had my friend Holly. Holly was my study buddy back when I was an undergraduate. One night we were on the phone prepping for the next day's exam on Jung's archetypes. It was about one-thirty in the morning and we'd exhausted every brain cell. I was lying on a floor littered with notes, the phone uncomfortably crooked between my neck and shoulder. I was tired and getting loopy. I knocked over a half-empty cup of coffee with my foot and absently watched it slowly soak into the carpeting before realizing I should be sopping the damn stuff up. I grabbed some stray notebook paper and began blotting. Suddenly Holly turned the rudder of our conversation. She told me how relieved she was that her husband was working the night shift. "At least I get a night off from him," she said. "He always wants sex."

"Really?"

"Every single day."

"Seven days a week?" Ridiculously, I started doing the math in my head until it was evident we were talking about a simple one-to-one ratio.

"I love him. But sometimes I can't stand it. Sometimes, I'll be lying there and tears are coming down my face."

"That's bad." The notebook paper wasn't efficiently absorbing the coffee. I wanted to excuse myself to grab some toilet paper, but that would make for an awkward and insensitive interruption.

"I think of leaving him, but then I can't. I just can't."

"Oh, Holly." I could feel her hurt all the way through the phone line.

"I know. I wish I had the guts. I need him. It's so pathetic. Sometimes I think he'll leave me. He works with this woman and I ask him what she's like, and he says she's attractive and, you know, they work closely together. I'm afraid if I turn him down for sex, he'll go get it from her."

Holly had tried creating mental desire, to think of sex as a gift she could give her husband. "I've tried to think of it as a way of showing my love and appreciation," she said. "But I still have these fantasies where he ends up in a wheelchair and I don't have to have sex with him anymore. I still have him. I still have the marriage. Isn't that just sick? And he's so grateful and I can love him again."

Holly began spending more and more time away from home. When I talked to her over the phone a couple years later, I asked if she had made some kind of peace with her sex life. "No, not really. I just stay away from him as much as I can." She went to her doctoral classes during the day, taught undergraduate classes at night, and carried on a nonsexual but very emotional affair with a co-worker. After nearly five years of marriage, Holly just plum ran out of gifts to give to her husband.

Therapists are notably silent on what months and years of giving in can do to a person, no matter how upbeat and positive she is. I would ask Love to simply travel back a few pages in her own book to a conversation she recounts between two men in group therapy:

> *In this particular group, whether the feelings of anger and rejection the men were experiencing were mild or intense seemed to depend to some degree on the length of the relationship. One of the men said that unlike the others, he wasn't upset when his girlfriend had no interest in sex. In fact, he took it as a challenge. He said, "That's when I get a grin on my face."*
>
> *"Yeah?" said the man sitting next to him. "How long have you been living together?"*
>
> *"Two years," he replied.*
>
> *"Well, come talk to me after you've been married thirteen years," he said grimly. "We'll see if you're still smiling."*

The same could be said for developing mental desire—a desire largely predicated on the theme of sexual gift giving. Birthdays and Christmas come but once a year, but try keeping the spirit of giving going two and three times a week, year after year . . . well, ladies, let's see if those smiles are still on your faces.

Seventeen

THE CHEMISTRY
BETWEEN US

I kept thinking back to my past looking for answers. All the guys I'd gone out with always had a higher sex drive than me. Some were more polite about it than others, but fending off—defense—was the usual game I played with men. Kip was definitely one of the kindest ones; others got termed "obnoxious." Obnoxious was my signal to my friends and others about how my dates went.

"Well, how did it go?"

"He was obnoxious."

Then they'd say, "Obnoxious how?" And I would launch into the liberties such and such thought he could take and so on and so forth. "Oooooh, yeah, I hate when they do that." Instant validation.

Gay men or straight men, it doesn't matter. Most want to get to the sex. Except gay men get more sex. Probably because they're with other men . . . and . . . ta-da! . . . around people with similar sex drives—that is, not women. Oh, but we so like to minimize any differences. And it's not just a little difference between men's and women's sex drives. It's big.

I think most people know that women have lower drives than men. It's a fact as hard and obvious as summer rain. But we now need it in writing and studies and statistics because, Dr. Love says, we have become very wary of biological generalizations when it comes to humans. It's PC to say that men and women have equal libidos since the sexes are supposed to be considered equal in all spheres, whether social, political, or sexual. But the opposite conclusion is pretty inescapable. As Love notes, "Even in these days when people scrutinize gender difference for any hint of bias, experts still maintain that biologically men are the more highly sexed gender." Ooooh, really? The more highly sexed gender? One, of course, couldn't tell by the complaints of the on-the-job pornographic surfing habits of men. Anytime they can get a break, it's on to Teenage Mutant Ninja Sluts.

MAXING OUT

Might not hormonal differences between men and women answer a heap of questions about why men are the way they are? Like why men will sleep with just about anyone who offers; like why men approach sex like a Hometown Buffet—they want endless variety and big heaping helpings; like why men can use any object as a fetish object; like why a man's dream come true is sleeping with all of the Dallas cowboys cheerleaders at once, while a woman's dream bacchanal is to shop, eat, and not gain weight.

The impact of male hormones on the sex drive is easy to see when a person undergoes a sex-change procedure from female to male. I was watching a documentary on gender bending. It involved commentary by Camille Paglia. And if you've ever listened to Ms. Paglia talk, you'd swear she was on speed or you were on downers. I kept having to rewind it just to catch what she was saying. She may have been saying brilliant things, but to me she sounded like speed dial. With relief, the film cut to a transsexual, Max Valerio, born Anita Valerio. Max was still in process, meaning she hadn't any surgery yet but was taking male hormones. Max described the effects:

> I felt [the effects of the testosterone injections] within the first three to four hours . . . It was an intense experience. The next day, when I woke up, I had so much energy. I couldn't believe how much energy I had! I was like, "Oh my God!" I went walking down the street, and I was thinking, "Is this how men feel?" I felt like I could run around the block ninety times! It was like rock and roll injected into my body!
>
> My sex drive went up after about a week and a half. And I thought I had a high sex drive before! And when people told me I would have a higher sex drive, I thought, "Well, how high could that be?" . . . It's like another world . . . Suddenly you understand why men tend to be more interested in pornography, why there's prostitution . . . of course! It makes sense . . . because sex is on my brain so much more of the time now!

The film showed Max, in a leather jacket, black jeans, and boots, walking down a street, punching the air and smiling, clearly happy with his new blast of energy. I could tell Max was going to make a great transsexual; he was definitely bad-boy handsome, good-looking enough for me to want to pick him up. The doses of testosterone this woman received were, of course, far greater than what a woman would receive to treat her low libido. For Anita to become Max, she had to have doses that would give her the physical characteristics of a biological male. And the results were impressive not only physically but libido-wise too.

But the most important thing I learned from Anita's story was the assumption made by her doctors. They told Anita that she would have a higher sex drive when given that large an amount of testosterone. They simply took it *for granted* that there was a direct correlation between high testosterone levels and higher libido. They didn't have to know how Anita felt emotionally, or the status of her personal relationships, or her confidence levels, or trust issues to know that the amount of testosterone she received would increase her sex drive enormously.

Anita apparently concurred. In the thirteen years since being in the film, Anita Valerio has now transformed herself physically as well as mentally into Max Valerio. He has not had "bottom" surgery but has been taking testosterone injections for over ten years now. His book, *The Testosterone Files*, is a fascinating memoir that takes the controversial position that hormones, not culture, are primarily responsible for the profound differences between the sex drives of men and women.

It's impossible not to notice that women don't feel a compulsive drive for sex. Men, on the other hand, have a continuous sex drive, an ongoing need that is easily aroused and not prone to die out with this or that distraction. I think that's why men always seem to be in a simmering state of sexual desire—almost any kind of sexual stimulation can inflame them—while women are more like a gas stove that needs to be continually reignited to create heat. No, actually that simile won't do; many women require more effort than lighting a match and turning on the gas. Getting a woman aroused and ready for sex is more like building a fire in the damp woods on a windy day. First you have to generate a spark and hope it catches the paper or little bits of grass, then you hope that it stays lit long enough to grab onto the kindling, carefully blowing on it and alternately sheltering it from too much wind, or the little flames will go out. And as we've seen, there are a multitude of things that may prevent a woman from even wanting to want sex, let alone going for arousal and climax. Many men, in contrast, can go from simmer to white hot in a heartbeat, and have a harder time cooling down when things don't pan out.

What explains these differences in desire between the sexes? Ockham's razor suggests we look to the simplest explanation first. So why can't we accept the simplest explanation, that hormonal differences mean that, in general, women have a lower drive than men? When the difference can be explained by human biology, why do we have to bring pathology into it? Women are not suffering from some sort of disorder. Bottom line, I believe it's hormonal hardwiring that primarily determines the strength of our drive for sex.

So, as far as sex goes, I'm prepared to accept that biology is destiny—somewhat. I must make a qualification. For instance, I read a column, "Date Girl," in an alternative weekly. One woman wrote that she has a very high sex drive, and her wonderful boyfriend has nearly none. I shall now type the word I truly fear: "counterexample." Those women *are* definitely out there, all along the sexual-desire curve. As far as biological appetites are concerned, I just happen to think a lot of us are huddled closer to the dessert than the desire end.

But even that statement may be too bold. Dr. Phil would surely put me in a headlock and smoosh my face straight into the camera lens (a fate I would oddly relish). The Bermans would tag-team counsel me until I confessed that my low libido was actually a defense mechanism designed to avoid joy. And if counseling didn't work, they'd rub testosterone cream onto my labia and then zap them with tiny heart paddles usually reserved for hamsters undergoing a cardiac event.

Never shall we admit that women have much lower sex drives than men. Never. I will be treated with drugs, psychoanalysis, spa-based encounter groups, warm rocks placed on my back, thong therapy, sex-toy parties, empowerment rituals, aromatherapy, and the advice to crash a *Girls Gone Wild* screening where I can hear *women* yelling, "Show us your tits!" As I end up in a straitjacket in a psych ward hopping about madly, I simply can't help noting the obvious. No one is trying to lower men's sex drives. I don't hear, "Doctor, my sex drive is *too high*. Please, do something about it. I feel guilty and ashamed that I don't want less sex. It's killing my marriage." I stop hopping after they give me my shot of Demerol and I lapse into a dream state. Wouldn't it be wonderful if men were urged to fall in line with women's sex drive rather than vice versa? Suddenly I feel myself floating above the *Oprah* show's stage, having a near-celebrity experience . . .

Eighteen

AN *OPRAH*
DREAM SEQUENCE

Here is *my* ideal *Oprah* show:

> OPRAH: We're talking to men today who say that their sex
> drive is endangering their marriages and damaging
> their self-esteem. The problem of abnormal sex drives
> is of epidemic proportions. Men everywhere are now
> coming forward to reveal a very embarrassing secret:
> their obsessive need for sex. Afraid that their wives will
> leave them, men are now seeking help with ways to
> lower their libidos. We will discuss psychological and
> physiological reasons that lead men to use sex as a
> substitute for love and self-esteem. And I don't want
> you to feel alone; millions of men are quietly suffering
> the same fate. But we're here to tell you there *is* help.

BERMAN & BERMAN: Sex can be a quick fix. A temporary high. Men use sex as a way to burn off anxiety and stress instead of getting to the root of it. Sex is a way to put off facing problems that may require lifestyle changes. The need for frequent sex (that is, more than an occasional indulgence a couple of times a month) is typical of avoidance behavior, whether in dealing with on-the-job stressors, family life, or intimacy with your partner.

OPRAH (VOICE-OVER): Experts say that men use sex in order to avoid intimacy. Their inability to connect with their partner in ways that are nonsexual shows an inability to be emotionally vulnerable with their partner. Instead, they substitute physical closeness for emotional closeness. A man who is in a truly loving, open, and intimate in his marriage will need sex less.

DR. PHIL: There are also symptoms of intimacy avoidance and low self-esteem. While cuddling or caressing your wife, you become sexually aroused. Often this is due to an inability to be truly vulnerable with your wife. The emotional closeness that comes with such open displays of affection becomes too threatening, so a man may respond to this threat by sexualizing affection. In this way he can limit his vulnerability by turning affection into a purely physical response.

OPRAH (MORE VOICE-OVER): Wives everywhere are throwing in the towel. They no longer want to be subjected to what they see as their husbands' emotional immaturity and impetuous, controlling behavior. Can these men save their marriages?

. . .

OPRAH (LIVE): We have our two sister sex experts back
   with us again, Dr. Laura Berman and Dr. Jennifer
   Berman. And joining us will be none other than Dr.
   Phil. Yeah! We'll all be talking to Rod today. Thanks for
   coming, Rod, and being so honest about a problem that
   so many men are suffering from in silence. I know this
   must be hard for you. I can see it in your eyes—
   tremendous sadness . . .

ROD: I don't know what to do! I've tried everything:
   meditation, cold showers, soft music—but I'm still so
   sexually needy!

DR. PHIL: Rod, I hear you saying you tried everything,
   but have you tried reconnecting with your wife?

ROD: I'm just so stressed after a long day, I just want to
   come home and zoom, zoom, zoom. I don't feel like a
   man anymore, I feel like a provider, a worker.

DR. PHIL: What do you get out of that . . . that exhausted
   "poor me" provider role?

ROD: Get out of it? Nothing, I hate it.

DR. PHIL: I think it's your way of being controlling and
   avoiding having to truly listen to the needs of your wife.
   You claim you're so stressed by work, you just want to
   come home and have sex with your wife.

ROD: Yes, it relaxes me and makes me feel loved.

DR. PHIL: And how do you think it makes her feel when
   you come home sometimes twice or three times in *one*
   week wanting sex?

ROD: It makes her feel lousy.

DR. PHIL: Of course it does. It doesn't matter what

reasons or excuses you give for wanting frequent sex, you have to realize she has needs, too, and one of them means not servicing *you* at the end of the day. If you don't fill her emotional and intimacy needs, you're gonna drive her right out the door. End of story.

DR. JENNIFER BERMAN: We have a dual approach of handling the problem of male sexual overdrive. Therapy is often indicated and occasionally medication.

OPRAH: I hear that men are starting to be prescribed women's birth-control pills. Is that true?

DR. JENNIFER BERMAN: It is, because estrogen is now thought to be the "love" hormone since it promotes affectionate behavior without the unwanted sexual side effects we see in "testosterone neediness." With estrogen supplementation, men become less aggressive and controlling, and more affectionate, vulnerable, and loving. They are more concerned with their families' and their wives' emotional well-being.

OPRAH: That sounds wonderful, doesn't it, guys? But I hear it could give some men breasts—is that true?

DR. LAURA BERMAN: No, not at all—as long as they're monitored closely. This side effect is seldom seen, though it is irreversible when it happens. Obviously, therapy should be the first route. Men should be taught to focus on the affection they feel for their family instead of on sexual release. Some men may need intense therapy because they have been brought up to believe that sex is the only pathway to manliness and love.

OPRAH: Yes—manliness. That's a good point. Men have

been taught that sex and manliness go together. This is really a self-esteem issue, isn't it?

JENNIFER B: Absolutely.

LAURA B: I think it's ridiculous to assume—I mean, we're all human, so it makes no sense to assume that men are so much more sexually needy than women. Men don't have to accept this disparity. There is hope, there is treatment.

Six months later . . .

OPRAH: Okay, last year we were talking to Rod, who was having trouble with his sexuality. Hi, Rod, welcome back.

ROD: Hi, Oprah.

OPRAH: Okay, Rod, well, c'mon, tell us all—we're dying to hear. We've gotten an overwhelming response since we aired that episode. Thousands of men wrote in who have the same problem.

ROD: Well, Oprah, I can't—I just can't describe the difference. I feel like a man again. And I didn't have to use sex to get there.

LAURA B: We used a combination of medication and intensive therapy. We worked on Rod's low self-esteem and managed to channel his demanding sexual energy into something more constructive.

OPRAH: Wow, this is big, big, big.

JENNIFER B: Now Rod gets his feeling of manliness by being vulnerable to affection and not pulling back by inserting sex into the proceedings.

ROD: So now I can cuddle with my wife without needing

to—to, uh, ya know, sabotage things by sexualizing everything.

OPRAH: Sabotage. Yes, that's the perfect word. Men sabotage their love lives and marriages with sex, don't they? Whoa, that's big. But why would they do that?

LAURA B: Once again, it goes back to self-esteem. These men think they don't deserve the pleasures of love, affection, and a good marriage, so they sabotage it.

ROD: I can't say what this has done for me. I'm no longer [tears well up in his eyes] . . . I'm no longer afraid she's gonna leave me. I finally am a husband again, and a man.

OPRAH (TEARING UP): This is—y'all are making me cry.

JENNIFER B: We also found in Rod's case that his testosterone levels were too high. So we boosted the estrogen and lowered his testosterone levels through a chemical hormonal inhibitor. And no, he doesn't have breasts [laughs].

OPRAH (LAUGHS): Thank goodness for that!

JENNIFER B: Of course things aren't perfect. Rod still has some progress to make.

ROD: Yeah, sometimes I still want to bug my wife for sex, but now I recognize it's not a need, but a cheap fix and a desire to be controlling.

The camera pans over men in the audience who are nodding sympathetically.

OPRAH: Wow—a lightbulb moment.

ROD: It's such a change from what I once was. I can't believe that I used to cuddle with my wife and think it was not enough. Now I've learned the pleasure of cuddling, of affection, and how much closer it brings my wife and me together at the end of the day. It's so healing.

DRS. BERMAN: Uh-huh.

OPRAH: Please, I know there are estimated to be tens of millions of men out there with this problem. Men in fear of losing their marriages. Get Jennifer and Laura Berman's book, *For Dudes Only: Don't Let Sex Get in the Way of Love*.

Will it ever happen? Oh, I wish it would. I wish it wasn't the case that women are automatically considered the deviants for wanting less sex. I'm sick of sucking up to societal expectations that make me doubt if my nature is natural.

Why weren't men going out in droves to accommodate the lower sex drive of women rather than women always accommodating the higher sex drive of men? Why wasn't it men who were all nervous as get-out about putting too many sexual demands on their wives? I wondered why we were the ones who are encouraged to give in. Why we were the one's who risked irreversible side effects from taking male hormones that didn't even work for most women. Yet Kip, like most men, wouldn't even entertain the thought of taking female hormones to lower his sex drive. I'm telling you, it was beginning to tick me off.

Nineteen

MAUDE ABOUT
THE MEDIA

The whole sexual culture was ticking me off. One night I woke up and Kip wasn't there. I got up and saw the TV flickering in the living room. His insomnia again. I walked up quietly and saw he was watching an infomercial for *Girls Gone Wild*.

"Hey," I said, startling him. "I still don't get it. I'm not coming down on you, okay? But, really, how come you like this stuff? The lighting is bad, the production sucks, and don't you hate seeing absolutely feral groups of men belching up beer and crude remarks?"

Kip looked at me warily, wondering if he should even bother answering. But he opted to say what was on his mind. He told me that, in fact, he didn't like the wolf pack of men, but he liked the raw reality of it, the idea that there might be women hidden all around (maybe even in line at the grocery store) who would be happy to shed their clothes and do something nasty just for the fun of it. Girls who once seemed out of reach were now performing for the price of a T-shirt. Unlike the professionals of porn, these women were saying, *We don't need no stinkin' payment. Look at these babies*—WHOOMP!

TORN WITH PORN

My deep displeasure, shall we call it, really started in earnest several years back. Just a few months after Kip and I moved in together, I found a stash of pornographic magazines among his files and books. They don't have a word synonymous with "emasculated" that can be applied to women, but that's how I felt.

I won't kid you. I went down for the count.

How could I not know what this supposedly sensitive man really thought about women? It was degrading. He *knew* I couldn't stand pornography, so was he trying to stab me in the back for not giving him enough sex?

There were soft-core magazines like *Playboy* and explicit beaver-shot magazines. I want to tell you, I was *not* thankful that there wasn't *Hustler* or *Genesis* or something worse in the box. Indeed, the thought that it could've been worse didn't even enter my mind. This was bad enough. It was worse than bad. I lost it.

I got up and left, swinging out into the intense bright light of summer. Hot, hot, hot. The heat and the anger made my head pulse. I crossed the street, maneuvering through the construction signs and the dust and dirt in the baked-in ruts. I went into Rite Aid Drugs and bought a pop and a pack of cigs. Balancing a cigarette in my mouth, I unscrewed the pop. I gulped it down, flicked the ash off of my cigarette. I looked up and down the street. The heat was killer. No shade. There was really nowhere to go but home.

It was my day off, so I had a few hours to stew on it. I became a neurotic, jealous wreck. I couldn't stand that in myself. Neurotic I can accept. But jealous? And over two-dimensional women? It's sick and it's weak. All I know is this stuff has gotta go. I'm ready to blow. Who can compete with these—ugh, I hate the word—*nubile*, big-busted, lipstick-lesbian porn women? And where are their thighs? They have no thighs. Son of a bitch. I lit a third cigarette from the butt of the second. Chain-smoking is seriously bad, but I'm seriously a woman on the edge of a nervous breakdown.

It was after six now. I heard the key in the lock. I stubbed out my cigarette in a bowl that still contained the soggy remains of bran flakes from the morning. I was ready for him. I threw a magazine at the wall just as he came in. "How could you do this? How could you have that? You had to know I hate that crap."

Kip looked shocked. Then he picked up the magazine, glanced at it, and dropped it back down. He was mad. "You went through my things!"

"No, I went through your college folders. Old papers, huh? That's porn, baby."

"So?" he says. *So*—like I'm the one who has some 'splainin' to do. "I don't think I need to apologize for it."

"What?"

"This is part of my sexuality," he said. That was no excuse to sneak porn in under my roof. "So, you either accept it or you don't," he continued.

I couldn't believe it; he was giving *me* an ultimatum? "You know what? I don't accept it. How's that?" I said, clapping my hands together in that old gesture of finality.

"This is part of my sexuality," he repeated. "It took a long time for me to come to terms with it. I've already worked it through."

"So nice. But you certainly didn't tell me about it."

"I knew how you'd react." Kip threw his hands out toward me as if saying, *You see? I knew you from the get-go.*

"Of *course* you did, that's why you hid it."

He started nodding. "Yeah, I did. I struggled with it because I *do* know some women think it's degrading." Then he noisily pulled a chair out and plunked down, his arms crossed over his chest. "I understand, but I'm not going to apologize for it."

That was mighty smug. The *least* he could do was apologize for it. "Well, I think that about sums it up. You've made your position clear. So, I guess that's it. It's over."

His nonchalant attitude dissolved. "That's it? I don't want that to be it." He sat down on the edge of the bed and put his head in his hands. "I don't want that to be it. I don't." Tears were creeping into his eyes. I was surprised by that but nonetheless pissed, too.

I got out another cigarette, lit it, and walked out the door. I stood outside in the parking lot. The night was warm. I wished there was some private place to sit, but there wasn't, so I just sat on a curbstone, smoking my cigarette, watching mosquitoes swirl around the lot lights.

When I came back in, Kip was sitting on the bed, looking dejected. He said he wanted us to get over this horrible episode. He didn't really need the porn—he just used it to ride out the empty spans in our sex life.

"So, what're you telling me? If I had sex with you every day, you wouldn't need porn? I'm driving you to it, right?"

"No—well, sex every day—yeah, I probably would need porn a lot less." Thanks. My fault.

"Well, I'm sorry I'm not one of your horny chicks with the blowup boobs!"

We continued to argue over the subject, but then he got up, went into the kitchen, and grabbed a trash bag. He gathered together his porn magazines and shoved them in. He was going to throw them out to keep the peace in our household.

But I stopped him. "You can keep them until you go," I told him. I told him this so that they would serve as a reminder that would keep my resolve strong.

He looked at me and said with grave sincerity in his voice, "I don't want to go." I looked away from him and leaned against the wall. "Look, I know you're upset. I can see how it can upset you, or I guess, any woman," Kip said.

Kip can sympathize with why this material could upset me, or any woman, especially in a committed relationship, but he can't truly empathize. He can't feel the pain of it all, the sense of betrayal, the envy, the petty jealousy that I felt I had no right to, the inferiority, the ugliness of having to deal with it all.

"I said I'd throw them out. Okay?"

"Why? You ain't staying here. You're going, remember?"

Kip tried to engage me in conversation about his pornography and why he had it. I silently listened as I cleaned up the bedroom. That's when he first told me about his struggles with lust and morality. But after years, he concluded, he had finally made peace with himself.

"Well, how would you like it if I brought home male pornography?"

Kip looked at me strangely, then said, "Why would I care?" Typical guy.

Kip said he didn't need porn as much when he lived alone. "Now that I'm sleeping next to a woman in bed every night . . . some ways I'm more sexually frustrated now than when I was single."

For two hours I kept going at him. Finally, I said, "I don't want to feel responsible for your interest in porn. I don't want this laid at my doorstep so that your conscience can go scot-free."

"You know, Joan—I'm getting tired of not being sorry enough for you."

"Kip," I said, smiling and shaking my head as if he were a little boy. "Kip, I don't need your apology, I need you to *understand.*" I was hoping to get my moral authority back. But I could see it had already checked out of the Whipping Boy Motel and was shoving the keys back toward me.

"All right . . ." *Should I give him this?* . . . "I guess I led you to think I liked sex more than I did."

"Yeah," he said, looking at me cautiously, waiting for me to fling another nasty comment at him. But then, when he saw that I wasn't going to, he told me, "Well, even so, we were already in love with each other." He looked at me hopefully. "At least, I'm in love with you." It was hard not to be touched by that.

Yet I still found myself struggling to accept the porn. Much of pornography is an insult to women. Porn, even at its best, is more than embarrassing and often humiliating both for the consumer and for the models. Porn creates a poor role model for women and the industry is rife with drugs and desperation, no doubt because it has hovered outside the edges of legitimacy, and thus has avoided regulation.

Personally, some of these pictures forced my eyes down in shame of my own sex. That anyone would want to see a person depicted in a pornographic way caused me to feel confused, fearful, enraged, sad, and even against my will, jealous. That hurt. And I kept letting Kip know it.

"Look," he said. "I'm obviously never going to win this argument on moral grounds. It'll keep going on and on and on. Let's not do this, I keep telling you, it isn't worth it. Let me just throw it out, okay?" He sat on the bed with his head in his hands.

Though I didn't want the magazines in my home, the thought of throwing them out seemed a hollow victory. If Kip were to throw out his porn, I wanted him to do it of his own free will.

On the other hand, I wasn't close to satisfying his sex drive. And having sex when I didn't desire it would be as much a burden to me as lack of sex was to him. I wouldn't have more sex with him simply to keep pornography out of the house.

"Well, at least you don't get the mean-spirited stuff." If he did, if he had something like *Hustler,* that would be it. I could only despise a man who could read that kind of misogynistic rag. All porn, I quickly decided, is not equal. But Kip still had to weather my attacks and fits of outrage. And worse, my incredible vacillation on the subject; one minute I'd rant about how degrading and insulting it was, and the next day, I would espouse my understanding of men's desire for pornography. In truth, I'm weaker than my convictions. I didn't want Kip to leave. So, instead of putting the kibosh on all forms of porn, I began to delineate and define. Yet there had to be a line that couldn't be crossed. The point where pornography turned into outright misogyny.

And porn brought up another question. If men's sexual natures are so raw and promiscuous, why blow smoke and hide it? "I don't get it, if men are so fixated on sex, so obsessed, then why not just leave us alone instead of saying bull like 'You complete me.' "

"I told you," said Kip. "We want love and affection, too. C'mon, women and men fool each other. Women think they can keep up with the sex drive of a man as long as they love them, and men think they can keep their sexual interests confined to one woman."

"Well," I said, knowing what he said was both pitiful and true, "it's a bunch of crap, isn't it?" I was more upset that Kip and I had got caught in each other's denial and traps just like so many other couples. We weren't special at all.

Kip repeated, there's more to men than sex. "There's love, affection . . ."

"All right," I said hesitantly. "Maybe . . ."

AND THEN THERE'S MAUDE

When pornography was limited to Kip's own private stash, that was one thing. Now it's everywhere, twenty-four hours a day, like hour-long *Girls Gone Wild* commercials. Another reason to fear insomnia.

That's why I hate watching movies. "Is every woman's response to this man to get naked and maul him? For God's sake, he's like, what? Sixty-two? And she's a twenty-two-year-old astrophysicist already at the 'top of her field.' This is ridiculous."

"Do you want me to turn the movie off?"

"No, go ahead. We'll still watch it." Then I sighed heavily. Kip hit the remote and the screen went blank. "Hey, I said you could watch it." Kip stood up and went to the coat closet. "What're you doing?"

"I'm getting up, I'm going out, and I'm renting the Wonderful frickin' World of Disney. All right? Is *that* okay with you?"

I squinted at him. "What is your problem?"

"What is *my* problem?" he asked with showy incredulity.

"Yeah."

"Maybe I'm sick of living with Maude."

"Maude?" A fragment of the show's lyrics went through my head: *That uncompromisin', enterprisin', anything but tranquilizin', right on Maude!*

"You know, the old seventies TV show."

"I *know.*" I paused. Then I thought, *Finally, the mitts are off. C'mon, bring it on.* "Okay, let's hear it."

The anger he was feeling must have acted like a catalyst. His words came out in a torrent. Like lancing a huge boil: he was tired of it. Tired of my always having to point out how women are being overly sexualized everywhere. Yes, he said, he knew it was true. He understood. How many times did he have to say it? But by the same token, he was a man and he liked it and wanted to feel free to enjoy it. He at least wanted the freedom to experience it vicariously without feeling guilt.

He might enjoy his truckload of vicarious thrills, but I thought he should have a nice dose of guilt to go with it. Because I'm just that kind of woman.

OLD-SCHOOL FEMINIST RILES MAN

We stopped talking at that point and went our separate ways in the apartment. I simmered for a while in the bedroom, trying to read a book. After flipping through the pages loudly enough to be heard twenty feet away, I slammed the book down so as to leave no doubt about how mad I was. I stomped back into the living room. "So, I'm Maude. I'm this castrating bitch."

Kip rolled his head in a show of *here we go again.* "Not that. Why do you have to take it to some dramatic extreme? You're just . . . *controlling*, is all."

"What. How? Telling you to take your vitamins?"

"Telling me what I should think. How I should think about women and society and how I should react. Your nonstop complaining during a Victoria's Secret bra commercial or because there are women jiggling on TV. Or any show or movie with sex in it. I can't even watch a movie with you anymore."

"That's because the women are always the sex interest . . ."

"I know, I know. 'Twenty-year-old astrophysicists at the top of their field—' "

"Who are really there to get naked."

"*Every* movie is going to have sex scenes. You have to make political comments each and every time. It wears on me. I have this feeling of frustration and dread—and sometimes it's just sex. Just a simple sex scene and you're next to me on the sofa just ready to burst. Maybe you hate sex and that's why you hate women who show how much they want it."

"That is not true!" *Was it?*

"Then why can't you, just once, shut up about it? Each and every time you—"

"Because it's all over! Women keep tearing off their clothes, and literally launching themselves into sex suffices as their most commendable personality trait." Yes, that's what it was—not that I hated sex! Ha!

"That's your view. That's your opinion. I told you I understand. But I don't need to hear it again and again. I don't need to be told how terrible it all is. I have to agree with you or you just go berserk. You're always questioning, 'How can you like that? How can you look at her?' I can't have one dirty thought in my head. All this crap is about *me* having to become *you*. Yes, you're Maude—" He got up and walked out of the living room.

"Oh, then you must be Arthur," I said, following him.

He went into the bathroom and shut the door. He yelled out, "*Walter.* Arthur is the last name of the actress. Bea Arthur. Walter is Maude's husband."

"Are you sure? Because I could've sworn it was Arthur."

"Jeez, never *mind,*" he said through the door.

"But if I'm Maude then you must think you're Arthur-Walter."

"No," he yelled out. "I'm not that whining, spineless guy."

"Great, I get to be Maude and you don't have to be Arthur."

Kip came out of the bathroom with a look of thunder on his face. Well, actually, a light rainstorm. "Can we get off of *you* for a second? I'm tired of you coming down on me if I like women who act sexy. So what?"

I was stiffly indignant. But it was true. I remembered mocking Paris Hilton when Kip said casually he didn't think she was so bad. I said in an accusatory tone, "Not so bad means you like her. How *could* you like Paris Hilton?" That did not meet with my approval. He said he didn't see why everyone comes down on her.

"That's your type? Some rich, spoiled ditz who shows her—"

"Yeah," he said defiantly, "I *like* her. Maybe I like women like Paris!" It can't be her voluptuous looks—his usual type. It must be her *personality.* Well, if he could like a woman like that . . . my shadow opposite. Now, tonight, he let loose: "I can like who I like. You come down like a hammer. Even my fantasies should meet with your approval. I've told you before that I understand—I can sympathize with it. But there's only so much sympathizing I can do. I'm a guy, and I can't pretend I'm not. It's everywhere—I'm bombarded by it."

"Well, why didn't you marry someone like that? Hmm? Let's have it. Why did you settle for Maude?"

"C'mon, I didn't mean that literally."

"Ohhhh, yes you did," I said, wagging my finger at him. "You agree with me about society and feminism going to hell in a hand-basket, and you're secretly glad of it—isn't that right? Isn't that the thing you can't tell me? You love a lot of it and you don't want me knowing that because you think it'll make you look bad, or hypo-critical, or that I'll have a meltdown—and you resent me for it. That's why you compared me to Maude."

"It's not easy being a man in Joan's world."

"It's not easy being a woman in a *man's* world. This is your world. Your Disney World of fun. I don't have a place in it. I'm the killjoy, the buzz kill, the rain on your souped-up, hard-breasted pa-rade of women happy to play the do-me sex kitten for men's—" I stopped in midsentence. Oops, that came out with so much more bile and vitriol than I'd intended.

But it wasn't just personal. I was angry that being called Maude was now a disparagement. She was a character who was ground-breaking at the time. She was someone many women looked up to. A daring, strong woman who had an imposing presence instead of a frilly, apologetic one. Now it seems she is a dinosaur. Someone who men needn't even hide their contempt for and that women would probably snicker at as an example of dowdy, old-school feminism.

I myself hadn't thought of Maude in a very long time, and only dimly remembered the series. But the feel of her personality was indelible. I had fallen far short of being anything like Maude, something I might have considered a failing if I had taken the time to consider it. But now I'd discovered I hadn't fallen far short enough.

CANDY LAND FOR MEN, LOLLIPOPS FOR WOMEN

Most pitiful was that the suggestion that I was some kind of feminist revolutionary wasn't even true. I was plain and simple a reactionary. Since my teens, my iffy feminism had been selective, and then went comatose. I had worn microminis in junior high. In high school I had a T-shirt that said *Sticks and Stones Can Break My Bones but Whips and Chains Excite Me*. I wore fishnets in college. I had gotten hired for jobs because of my boobs instead of my personality or skills. I lived with a number of men who loved my false confidence and high-heeled boots and ended up treating me like crap.

I changed a lot after taking some consciousness-raising women's studies courses in college. But another reason, shameful to say, is that, more and more as I got older, traditional feminism had become my creed as I saw myself gradually being sidelined by women portrayed with aggressive sex drives, who go to strip clubs and buy their men lap dances—and even get them themselves. I hated being overshadowed in a world where tits and ass had replaced character. Character was no longer something a woman consciously desired, it was what one cultivated as a sad last resort when she lacked those bouncy physical attributes or welcoming sexuality that men tipped their hats and smiled for.

Twenty

GIRL POWER

Though I'm no fan of female sexuality as depicted on *Sex and the City*, the show was at least more empowering than *Girls Gone Wild*. I mean, I could see why women found this sex-and-shopping fantasy alluring—even if it seemed more gay male than straight female to some. We're not repressed, hesitant prigs. We're lusty, vivacious, and a little dangerous. And watch out, mister. The next ass that's leered at just might be *yours*.

Why, in the words of Henry Higgins, can't a woman be more like a man?

Suddenly I'm Carrie sitting in Jimmy Choo's pondering a $499 pair of shoes. Ooooh, it's going to bust my budget, but who could resist? A girl needs a little lift now and then. I wear my ridiculously impractical shoes home. Run a brush through my long blond hair.

Grab the Prada handbag that matches my new kicks, then head out
to O'Neal's, where I'm meeting my posse. Charlotte, Miranda, and
Samantha already have a head start on their Cosmopolitans. But
given the way I click along the varnished wood, *everyone* stops what
they're drinking, doing, or saying to look down at my shoes.

"Okay, what's going on south of your ankles, Miss Lady?"

"Oh my God, is that Jimmy I see?"

"How, much? No. Don't tell me. Three hundred and seventy-
five dollars?"

"More?"

"Four hundred?"

"Four hundred and ninety-nine."

"I thought you said you weren't going to spend any more money
on shoes!"

"Well, okay. What else can you do when the love of your life
keeps wreaking havoc with your love life?"

"Yeah, what happened? Another Mr. Big argument leave you
high and dry?"

"I completely lost my shit with Big over the phone."

"Carrie, you've got to learn how to play him like he's playing
you."

"The only place a woman has complete control of a man is in
bed."

"Yeah, and you've got to get him *into* bed to see what he's really
got going on."

"It seems you can't swing a Fendi tote without hitting a loser."

"Why don't you just leave him, Carrie?"

"Because the sex is so, urrgghhhh!" (Closing her eyes and
groaning.) "It's so awesome, you wouldn't believe it."

"Awesome sex."

"Wow, you can't say no to that."
"Or to a fantastic pair of shoes."

DATE LIKE A MAN, BUT . . .

Independent, snazzy, sexy, lustful, and sexually voracious women are not just found on *Sex and the City*, they are also staring out at us from the covers of women's magazines, television sets, and movie screens. They are feminists and therapists, starlets and movie stars, supermodels and soap actresses, sitcom moms and sitcom daughters, and all those hot, hard, stylish career girls us rubes can't imagine. They're giving women advice in magazine columns and talk shows.

Relationship expert Myreah Moore would seem to be following that smart tigress path. Especially considering the title of her popular book *Date Like a Man*. In it there's a section with the bold title "How to Have Sex Like a Man." But very curiously, the majority of the chapter deals with what men want sexually, not women. Here are some of the headings:

Men Like Blow Jobs
Get to Know Mr. Happy
Kiss It, Lick It, Squeeze It, Tease It
Deep Throating
Men Like Women Who Swallow
Men Like Pornography
Men Like Lingerie
Men Like to Talk Dirty
Men Like Women Who Bring on the Noise

Men Like Women Who Are Flexible
Men Like Lesbians

Moore wants women to see sex through a man's eyes as a great way to keep him coming back for more.

In one of my favorite passages, Moore suggests another way to keep the heat sizzling for your man: accompany him to a strip bar. "While you're there, buy him a lap dance." Hey, wait a minute. What about dating like a man and making him service our sexual needs and cater to our interest and all that jazz? Isn't that's what the *Sex and the City* phenomenon is all about? And even if I don't find these women typical, I figure if you always have to play the girl in these sex wars, it shouldn't mean you're always the one on your knees.

TRY IT, YOU'LL LIKE IT

According to *Cosmo,* women are supposed to love being on top, stripping, and playing with themselves in front of men. (Oh, yes— it was my glamour mags not porn that first put me wise to that technique.) You can slowly build on that list by adding more and more variations and, when comfortable, experimenting and exploring even more so neither partner gets bored. "Truly amazing erotic action can happen only when both partners are willing to take risks," says Catherine Liszt, in *When Someone You Love Is Kinky.* "When you go beyond your limits, you discover hidden sensations and new turn-ons." Kinkiness apparently is not a problem requiring counseling or even, minimally, a funny look. Rather, it's opportunity come a-knocking for the unkinky partner (a "Mary Poppins," as

Cosmo puts it), who now has the good fortune of expanding her sexual horizons. We are presented with an endless parade of something that we have to try "just once" or risk being seen as withholding and spiteful.

Pamela Lister, while an editor at *Redbook* magazine, coauthored the book *Married Lust,* which quotes a woman who is tired out by her husband's need to sexually experiment. She feels nagged and pressured by his repeated requests but says, "I have agreed to all of his experiments but on my own schedule. I'd like the space to think about them without being made to feel inadequate or prudish. He obviously has spent time on the matter. I expect to be allowed to do the same." Her husband spends considerable time thinking about acting out *his* fantasies while she presumably needs time to gulp and steel herself to the idea of another new kink.

This is the position that so many women are in. Lister cautions that you shouldn't feel pressured to perform a sex act you don't want to do. For instance, on the subject of anal sex, Lister says:

> *One of the reasons therapists think anal sex has come into its own (besides Marlon's buttery influence) is that it's become a very common and a very strong focus of pornography. Guys see it on film all the time. That's great. But porn, as we know, is fiction. You are real. And if you don't want to do what fictional women do, you shouldn't.*

Yet, that being said, she thinks you should at least try everything once. Even though she cites experts who say that most couples quit their experimentation with anal sex because it causes the woman "discomfort," and find the hygienic aspects distasteful, you should nevertheless try it at least once. "Even if you hate it and never do it again, chances are you two will be proud to have charted new territory together." Still, according to Lister, once may not be enough for some experiments. She says we may need time to know if something is going to work or not.

Maybe I was simply being old-fashioned. I didn't think twice about giving a blow job; I found it gets you a great table at a restaurant. But it, too, used to be thought of as exotic. Now anal *is* the new oral.

Lister believes women should be open to new sexual adventures. Instead of saying no, we are encouraged to be flexible. She says if your husband proposes a new sexual adventure or kink he's seen in pornography, remain open to it. She also says needing reassurance and talking about the pros and cons of doing this or that sex act is fine, but not if it gets in the way of actually doing it. Lister remonstrates those women who dillydally: "At some point, though, the talk has got to stop or you might ruin the walk. As this frustrated husband describes: 'Too often, the moment is spent talking about the how and why and why-nots of trying something new instead of just doing it.'"

It's obvious to me that if women are going through all the details and pros and cons of a sexual "experiment," it's because they don't feel good about it. Telling women, in effect, to get over it is tantamount to bullying them into kinky sex. The reason so many of us are "frustrating" men when it comes to kinky sex is that we don't feel we have the right to say no outright, so we try to get lost in the details of the act, the feelings that may be involved, the physical stress, any emotional repercussions, and so on and so forth. We are procrastinating, looking for a loophole, waiting for that last-second call from the governor.

FEMINISM GONE WILD

I didn't want to be prude girl. The girl that made all the other girls giggle and the boys turn away. I felt ashamed and secretly ostracized from society and my own sexuality. Not unlike that gay pro football player I saw on TV. My shame would remain for years until I came across Ariel Levy's book *Female Chauvinist Pigs*. In the book, Levy follows the rise of "raunch culture." It's a culture that is being nourished and perpetuated, ironically, by females. And sometimes, in the very name of feminism. I kissed the hot-pink cover of that book and danced around the kitchen with it. It didn't deal with female libido. But Levy took a very hard and, I think, brave look at what passes for the public representation of female sexuality. My shame at not being the hottest, coolest, grooviest chick on the block (or sadly, in my own apartment) was lifted enough to dissipate some of that black cloud that hung over me.

Levy is a reporter who has followed around the crew for *Girls Gone Wild* and *Maxim's* search for the "Hot 100" and went behind the scenes of the *Man Show* and other various places. I think the most interesting part of her book is her thesis that many women, in the name of feminism, have helped develop a raunch culture that takes on and celebrates the meaner male forms of sexual objectification. Out of the many examples Levy cites, her experience with CAKE serves as one of the most hard-hitting.

CAKE, a slang term for female genitalia, is an organization founded by Emily Kramer and Melinda Gallagher. Levy cites Kramer explaining that CAKE promotes female sexual culture: "'CAKE's mission is to change public perceptions about female sexuality,' and their Web site claims they seek to 'redefine the current boundaries [of] female sexuality.'"

That sounds wonderful, until you actually see it in practice at CAKE's famed parties, which, Levy writes, are prominent enough to have been featured on a 2004 episode of *Law & Order* under the name "tart parties." During CAKE parties, strippers, *female* strippers, are hired for some of the stage shows. Some of these are known as the CAKE dancers. As women in thigh-high boots, fishnets, and tiny bras mounted the dance stage, Levy watched the celebration of female sexual liberation:

> *At first, they shimmied onstage like garden variety lusty club-goers. But then a visiting crew from Showtime turned on their cameras and when the lights hit the dancers they started humping each other as if possessed. A blonde woman with improbably large breasts immediately bent over and a dancer with a souped-up Mohawk got behind her and started grinding her crotch against the other woman's rear end.*

As Levy watched, "Many, many men formed a pack around the stage and most pumped their fists in the air to the beat of the music and the humping." Yet CAKE bills its parties as "feminism in action," promoting "female sexual culture." As comedian Kathy Griffin commented, "Paris is the new Gloria Steinem." I believe it. After watching a CAKE party, Levy writes, "Despite what can fairly be called a campaign of begging on my part, Kramer and Gallagher refused to answer questions about why they can't achieve their 'female-directed sexual revolution' without the constant presence of taut, waxed strippers."

Levy gives us a take on these proceedings: "When I'm in the plastic 'erotic' world of high, hard tits and long nails and incessant pole dancing—whether I'm at a CAKE party, walking past a billboard of Jenna Jameson in Times Square, or dodging pillows at the

Maxim Hot 100—I don't feel titillated or liberated or aroused. I feel bored, and kind of tense." When you're deriding young women who love showing it off, you're definitely a prig. "Raunch culture, then, isn't an entertainment option, it's a litmus test of female up-tightness." The eternal question posed by so many men *and* a new crop of women is, If those girls don't mind, why should you?

But this is not my playland, not my sexuality. This is for the boys. Levy speaks out on what I had been initially afraid to say: that this culture of unbridled male fantasy has been co-opted by women in the name of feminism and sexual liberation. That's why it's so hard to criticize it—because you're attacking what women have supposedly been striving for for decades. And the shame of being denounced is real. From academia to the street, there is a great stake in presenting female sexuality as always robust. But Levy sees that in the new raunch culture, men are still the gold standard. They still get to define our sexuality.

My sex drive couldn't ride the huge cultural sex wave that kept coming in. Instead I was being beaten against the beach. The culture had turned, and there was no way to push the tide back. The sexperts, the pro-family traditionalists, the feminists, and the skin peddlers of the media were all on the same side now, hoping to tug my sexuality in a more lustful direction to sell their products, save my marriage, or make their point.

I couldn't deny Kip's needs. But neither could I, as much as I wanted to, make myself sexually devilish and proactive without a sex drive to go with it. I knew too much about myself to kid myself (right then, these insights were more of a cruel irony than a blessing).

So I quit fighting. I quit less out of principle than out of resignation. This is how it is. What else was there to do?

DIRE WARNINGS

Of course, if I gave up on sex, there would be repercussions for my marriage. In *Date Like a Man*, Moore warned women they have to pay lots of oral attention to "Mr. Happy" or risk losing their man to a woman with a more receptive mouth:

> *Giving head can be fun because men love it so damn much and because you are in control of his pleasure. If you find this activity distasteful, guaranteed he will find someone who thinks his dick is Cherry Garcia on a sugar cone. The truth is, honey, a man doesn't care who's down there. It could be a man, a robot or a succubus. All they know is that it feels good. Besides, he can't see your face anyway.*

Whoa! That's harsh. That and the fact I couldn't get over her calling it Mr. Happy.

Then I remember Mo'nique. She starred on the sitcom *The Parkers* and was on a stand-up tour with *The Queens of Comedy*—and she had plenty to say about sex and men. She is a counterexample to any argument that says the only women who have unwanted sex are those looking to keep hold of financial security. Mo'nique is the financially successful half of her marriage. Foulmouthed, raucous, bawdy, aggressive, and not afraid to bash social standards, Mo'nique takes on a surprisingly submissive and traditionalist stance when it comes to men. She has a message for the women in the audience: a good man is hard to get and worth doing your utmost to keep. She bemoans the fact that so many women are losing their men out of pride and a stubborn unwillingness to please them. Especially when it comes to the bedroom:

As a wife I still know my place with my husband; even
though I make all the money, he's still king of the castle. I
give him what he wants when he wants it. I would not lose
my shit over things I won't do when it comes to the bedroom.
He calls me the FBIA—the Freakiest Bitch in America
because I give it to him however the f—— he wants it. And
for you crazy bitches talking about "I ain't gonna do
that nasty shit. I ain't gonna do that freaky shit," let me tell
you something: What you won't do, another bitch will. And
she'll do it so swell he won't come back. So if your man wants
to do some nasty-ass, gutter butt, trifling, slutty, ho-ish,
pornographic bullshit—you better get with the motherf——-
ing program, baby!

Naturally, we must allow for the exaggerations of comedic license. But I believe she was serious about her message. Mo'nique
wears sexual compliance to male demands like a badge of honor.
She's woman enough to take just about anything her man can
dream up and dish out. She's got a husband and if you don't it's because you put your pride before your man.

Cancún Cuties, Desperate Housewives, Cherry Garcia . . . on
a cone. The more I think of such imaginary scenarios, the more I
get mad. What if Kip ends up in a strip club? Like the one just behind me.

I'm standing at First and Union, waiting on a bus. In back of
me is the Lusty Lady. Strippers, nude dancers, lap dances—I don't
know which variety of "live" entertainment they're selling, maybe
all three. Dozens of little lightbulbs decorate the huge pink sign,
flashing in a waving rhythm. Beside me, a young woman with
smoky eyes and tight leather pants leans against a wall. She's also
waiting on the bus. Guys go by and twist around to look at her. I

shrug inside my trench coat. I feel dull and nonsexual. Everywhere I go, I contrast myself to the sexual heat that plays from every corner of the city. I feel reproached by the seedy yet sexual pulse of Seattle. Half scorning the Lusty Lady and half frightened by her, I repeat to myself that I'm not, I'm not, *I'm not* a sexless loser.

LOSING MY COMPASS

I had run out of options. Kip and I had gone to a sex therapist and that didn't help. Some things raised my interest in sex temporarily simply because whatever it was provided me with an illusion of hope that it would work to muscle up my libido. I had tried giving sex as a gift, looking at sex as a spiritual act, thinking naughty thoughts and simulating lust, engaging in quickies, acting spontaneously, and trying for better orgasms. None of it had an appreciable effect on my sex drive.

And once again, I went further and further down the slide. Again, I began to not so subtly put sex off. All told we went from sex once a week, to once every two weeks, to less than once a month, and less . . .

Twenty-one

GOING PLATONIC

Kip was the first one to openly acknowledge it. We had just turned out the light and gone to bed. He tossed around a few times.

"Can't sleep?"

"No."

"How come? Is it your shoulder?"

"No . . . I just . . . I'm thinking. I'm thinking we should . . . we might as well be platonic. You know?"

I didn't say anything. I waited.

"I don't like to be in limbo. I need to have things clear cut. Why don't we agree this is a platonic marriage. Okay?" I held my breath and stayed perfectly still. He sensed my shame, my worry. But he also must have noticed I didn't jump in to vociferously protest. "It's okay, really, it'll be all right. I still love you. That's not gonna change."

"Are you sure?" I was both relieved and anxious.

"I've got my pornography," Kip told me. "That'll be enough."

Pornography had been acting as a decent supplement to our sex life when the sex was more infrequent than Kip could comfortably tolerate. I knew he didn't want to be increasingly dependent on porn. At the same time, he didn't want me to be overwhelmed by his sex drive. He had thought we could both improve our sexual intimacy at the same time. It didn't happen.

Pornography had worked well enough as a supplement, but could it carry the burden of being a total, ongoing replacement for sex?.

Kip said it would.

"No, how could that be enough?" I asked.

"It was enough when I was in college. It'll be okay. Really, it will be enough. I love you. I don't want sex to come between us."

I suspected his sense of duty was so honed and high-minded, he would never forgive himself for divorcing me over sex. But I didn't want him to stay with me out of a sense of duty—what a dulling, deadly blow to a marriage. He adamantly reassured me that wasn't true. "No, I want this to work. We've come this far."

"No, you're having that same sword fight you had with pornography when you were born-again, but now you're having it with me. You still think you can rise above lust and transcend upward to a pure, chaste love. It's a discipline thing for you, or some kind or pride thing—I don't know. This time you think you can win."

"You don't have to listen to what I say. You don't have to believe me. But I'm telling you, it isn't that. I'm not going to tell you a lie. If you think I'm lying, great, forget it."

"I think you're lying to yourself."

"You would be wrong. I know myself. If I didn't want to be with you because of sex, I wouldn't be with you. Pornography will be just fine for me—and as long as you accept that, we can do this."

"Look, don't martyr yourself," I said snottily, I think to compensate for the weak decision I was about to make. I wanted to believe him. I wanted to believe we could have a marriage without sex and still have a loving, happy Kip. I wanted to stay married.

"I'm a lot stronger and I've got more integrity than you think," he said.

Well, I thought, Kip might be congratulating himself on his nobility right now, but wait a few months. He was going to crack. And after seven months, crack he did.

It came like a punch in the stomach. Kip announced he didn't want to sleep in the same room with me. "I've been thinking and I think it would be best if we slept in separate rooms," he said one evening. I was sitting down, looking up at him as he stood by his desk. I didn't comprehend what he was saying at first. "I need somewhere I can be alone . . ." Tears sprang to my eyes. He said, "It's no big deal. I just need my own space." It was a cliché, but I knew there were no words that would say it any better. I didn't ask why. Instead, I hunched over my legs with my head down, elbows resting on my knees, my hands clasped together. I was trying to hide. But, oh God. The tears kept coming, dropping off my cheeks onto my pants and the carpet. "I still love you," he said quietly. I acknowledged this by nodding silently. But I didn't believe it.

I clearly remember when Kip's friend Jack and his wife, Debbie, began having marriage trouble. They thought it might help if they slept in different rooms and acted like they were dating. But it didn't work; they filed for divorce a few months after. Kip had said before he thought the demise of their marriage was hastened by their sleeping in different bedrooms. I remembered his exact words: "When you start doing that," he had said, "you'll kill the intimacy right there." Dammit. He knew what he was doing.

Kip put his hand on my shoulder, but I pulled away, saying, "It's okay, it's okay. Just let me have a minute alone." He walked to the bathroom and brought back a swath of toilet paper. My nose was running. I took it from his hand but didn't look at him. He went into the bedroom and shut the door. It was then that I gave in to myself. I grabbed a pillow off the couch and buried my face in it, sobbing uncontrollably.

A few minutes later he came back out, sat down next to me, and said he couldn't continue to sleep with me in the same bed and not feel keenly frustrated. He repeated the same thing: How could he deal with me lying beside him every night and yet not think of sex? On top of it, he said I liked to cuddle with him, but didn't I realize how hard that makes it for him? Put the shoe on the other foot, he said. How would I feel if he refused to cuddle or hug me, day after day, week after week? I thought to myself, *That's bull—it must go deeper than that.*

I got on my coat, snatched up my old, scrungy ski cap, put a couple of bucks in my pocket, and walked out the door. I had no idea where I was going but I needed to get out of our apartment. I took the stairwell instead of the elevator, decreasing the chance I'd meet anybody. I banged open the front door of the building and ran out into the cold.

Well, what're you going to do? I asked myself. *I'll walk and debate all choices until I can come to a decision. Do I want my mar-*

riage to survive? Of course. What can I do? What am I willing to do? I wasn't ready to answer that question.

BREAKING UP IS HARD TO DO

Though things hadn't been right between us for some time, I had still been stunned by Kip's cool declaration. Having only a one-bedroom apartment meant only one of us would stay in the bedroom. He wanted his own space, so I agreed he should have the bedroom as his retreat. It had a door you could shut and it seemed that's what he wanted. I'd sleep on the futon in the living room. Immediately he started moving most of his stuff into the bedroom. His computer and desk. His chair. File cabinet. The stereo. A week later he bought his own TV and DVD player. It had really hit the fan.

Once Kip moved into the bedroom, he totally distanced himself from me at the very time I most needed reassurance. In the evenings and on the weekends, he sequestered himself in the bedroom, only coming out for a bite to eat now and then. The days slipped by and I alternated between walking around like a robot and shamefully crying my eyes out at coffee shops because I was too afraid to be alone.

HOW FAR WOULD I GO?

I thought to myself, *All right, let's be rational. Think. What's the worst that could happen?* After moving to Seattle, the great jobs we thought were waiting for us suddenly fell through. After a couple of months of papering the city with applications, Kip landed an entry-level job as a quality control tech and I got a job as a leasing agent. Not high-status jobs. Suffice to say that neither of us was making enough money that a split wouldn't be very hard financially on both of us. But at least Kip had the support system of his family here. I didn't. If we split up, I'd still have the leasing job. But little money. I'd have to find another job.

What about psychologically? Yes, if things took a turn for the worse, I'd be devastated. Either way, I'd have to go back to Cleveland. I had friends there who might take me in for a while. Second, I wouldn't be able to bear living here in a city I was still a stranger to and that would be the site of the total disintegration of my marriage. But somehow, I'd survive. Okay, now I was getting somewhere.

I knew I couldn't have unwanted sex with Kip as part of any survival strategy, personal or financial. Not that I'm above it. I'm just a bad liar when it comes to that. I'd be so full of resentment that I'd probably pop in a matter of weeks. And I remembered my friend Holly, giving in to her husband after night after night because she was convinced he'd leave her if she didn't. And there was Michelle. Her husband had cheated on her a couple of times and it was her fault. He got bored. If only she had . . . fill in the blank. What's the use—as far as sex is concerned, men are always going to want more than a lot of us can deliver.

BE MY VALENTINE

February 14 rolls around and I dread it. I don't want any guilt-laden valentines. It means nothing. Inside, I've curled up like a potato bug into a shiny ball. And that's the way I want to keep it. I let my anguish solidify into blank looks and monosyllables. I think about past Valentine's Days: reliably romantic in the classic sense—flowers, chocolates, dinner, a little bauble. In less troubling days, I found this charming. I was in the in-club on Valentine's. Safely ensconced in a permanent relationship with my affectionate and kind husband.

What had been my gift to him? What would he want? Right, sex. My gift had always been showering, exfoliating, shaving, and trimming. Perfume? *Check.* Hair sculpted with spray? *Check.* Makeup? *Check.* A look of sweet lasciviousness? *Check, check.* The romance both pleases and reassures me, but also brings a sense of quiet obligation. It's the same obligation that always loiters in my mind, not any pressure applied by Kip. If I have been lax in the sex department, now was the time to make reparations. And it's a good time to do it. A night of lingering passion for him, of candlelit romance for me. Valentine's Day doesn't make me any hornier, but the sexperts are partly right—a woman does need to feel loved and special to have sex, but that doesn't mean that she feels any more pure lust, a strong physical urge to have sex. Instead, it makes her more *receptive* to having sex. As Patricia Love might say, feeling loved gives us the generosity to bestow on a man the gift of our bodies.

But not this year.

Yet . . . there's an envelope. It's a card, but not the kind I anticipated. Over the past couple of years, the card was your basic drugstore variety, with a hastily scrawled *I love you.* This one was handmade, with a beautiful message written in Kip's calligrapher's pen. The card had also been hand-decorated with heart-shaped metal studs, sparkling glitter, and washes of color. It must've taken some time to do this. I hadn't gotten a card like this since we were dating (he always made me handmade cards back then). I was touched and confused.

I say, "It's beautiful." That's true, but a part of me resents being jolted out of my protective cocoon. I'd been going through all of the Kubler-Ross five psychological stages of losing something you love, in this case, my marriage. I was feeling mighty low, but I was certain "acceptance" was just round the corner. Having to acknowledge that Kip put a surprising amount of thought and care into that card caught me off balance. It brought a sad nostalgia that rocketed me back to the first teary shock of grief.

Kip is hovering, waiting for me to say more. I simply say, "I'm surprised." I look at him pointedly.

"Why?"

Oh God. Doesn't he get? Could he be that clueless or is he deliberately ignoring the obvious—trying to assuage his guilt. I sigh in frustration. Yes, he's going to make *me* drag out the monsters from under the bed. "Why? Because we haven't been exactly getting along. At all."

"I still love you."

"You moved into your own room, your own bed, your own everything."

"I need the space, that doesn't mean I don't love you."

I want to bash my head repeatedly on the coffee table. "We don't even talk like normal people anymore, okay? You're gone even when you're here." I won't take the succor he's offering me. "You used to make me these cards—these handmade cards—then it all started going downhill."

"We've had some great Valentine's Days."

"Yeah."

"Remember when we went out to Heck's for dinner and then drove to Edgewater?"

Sure I remember. It was a clear, brittle, cold night. We got out of the car and huddled together looking out over Lake Erie and the lights of downtown Cleveland. An often dreary city by day, it was as pretty as any city when lit up in the night. Yes, it was the quintessential Valentine's Day. We ended the evening with sex. A nice end to a wonderful evening. Though this romantic postcard floats in front of my eyes, I recognize that the sex was still more of a loving accommodation I was happy to give rather than a response to physical desire.

I said softly, "Yeah, we had a good time."

"Sex was good then, wasn't it?"

I paused. How could I betray a memory? "Yeah. Yeah."

"So what's so different now? I thought I've been a pretty romantic guy."

"No, no—I don't expect all that. I don't know . . ." I pause in midsentence. I suddenly feel hot and strangled by my sweater. I pull it up and over my head and rip it off angrily. I want to rip everything to pieces. I'm sick of all the whats and wherefores. I'm sick of the sniveling half lies I tell. Sick of the shame.

I feel out of control. But I let the anger keep rising because it's better than feeling pathetic.

I stand up and pace the floor for a minute before deciding to go into the kitchen. Using my arms, I leverage myself up onto the counter. I twist over onto my knees and slide my way across to the last cupboard. I reach up to the very top shelf and feel around for the pack of cigarettes. I barely snag it with two fingers. I jump back down and grab some oven matches. I walk past Kip and slide open the glass door to the balcony. Leaning over the railing, I light my cigarette. It's stale as hell. I've had the same pack of cigarettes for eight months now.

I stare down at the alley. A pickup drives up, stops, and a man gets out. He throws three or four large garbage bags into our Dumpster, hoping to do some illegal dumping. I call out to him, "Hey, HEY!" He looks up and gives me the finger. I yell, "I got your license plate, you fool!" That stops him. He pulls the bags back out and drives off. I take a long drag off my cigarette and consider the empty alley.

I put the cigarette out on the metal railing and throw the butt into an old flowerpot. I take a deep breath then walk back into the living room. I announce, "I'm never going to be what you want sexually."

"What do you think I want?"

I decide to skip all the quantitative angles like how many times and how long and go right for the qualitative core: "I think you want someone who'd enjoy sex as much as you do—or close enough. I'm nowhere near that."

"I know, I know. Well, that doesn't mean we have to give up on the marriage. There're probably a lot of couples that live in a sexless marriage. And we were friends first. You're still my friend."

He looks at me with what he thinks is sympathy, but I see only pity and look away. I remember some old self-help advice: if you want to know how a man really feels about you, don't listen to his words—look at his actions. Kip's actions say he wants to be apart from me. As soon as he comes home, it's dinner then straight to his room. Another side of me thought maybe he did still love me. Maybe what he said was the truth—it was his sexual frustration that had prompted the move. But could it have such a *global* effect on our relationship? I hardly saw him during the week and then on weekends he stayed in his den/office/bedroom most of the day with the door shut. What was that about? If it was just the sexual frustration of sleeping with me in the same bed and not having sex, well, that would be one thing, we'd just sleep apart. But we were hardly spending any waking moments together. It couldn't only be sex.

Then I thought about the time he asked me to imagine the reverse: What if he never wanted to hug or hold me or show me any other kind of physical affection like kissing my cheek or holding my hand? How would that make me feel? I thought hard about this. It would feel like he didn't love me, no matter what excuse he gave—I'd still feel that deep down, touching me made him recoil. Definitely a love spoiler. It made me rethink some of what I'd read in the self-help books by the likes of John Gray and Patricia Love. Maybe men do feel shamed and rejected by wives who don't want sex with them. I just thought it irked the hell out of them—no nooky! It doesn't help that women have witnessed men treat sex so casually, separate from love. I thought accessible sex was simply a handy perk of marriage for a guy. But if I put myself in his shoes and switched the needs around, lack of nonsexual physical affection would leave me feeling incredibly rejected.

But even this understanding wasn't any help to me. I couldn't—I wouldn't—have sex with him as an obligatory "gift" just to keep him from leaving the marriage, not even after a night of romance. (And not the "romance" you put in quotes because it's a euphemism for sex; I mean the genuine article, the chaste, chivalric romance of yore, whenever that was.) And though I made a parallel example of sex and cuddling, they are categorically different. Having unwanted sex will poison a marriage. You feel used in the most intimate way possible. I wasn't going back to that. It wouldn't save my marriage but simply prolong its death.

So I stood with my arms crossed, a residual buzz of nicotine still thrumming inside my head. There was nothing left to say. I dismissed any further discussion by plopping down so hard on the sofa that a cup of coffee sitting on the coffee table sloshed its contents over the rim. I picked up the cup, ignoring the crescent-shaped puddle, and watched TV with the sound off.

Twenty-two

THRASHING IT OUT

A few more sodden Seattle months went by. I wore sweaters over sweaters, trying to shake the chill. I shrank back into myself, eyeing Kip with wariness whenever he was friendly to me. Most of the time, he was painfully polite. An anxious melancholy had overtaken me. I jumped every time the phone rang—staring at it until it would stop. But after a while, as more and more of nothing happened, I began very slowly to take another look at our little problems.

MEETING HIM HALFWAY

Was there any give to my position? At first there didn't seem to be. I either wanted sex or I didn't. I wasn't about to have sex when I didn't want it. How could I find a way in which sex wouldn't be a burden to me? Finding an answer was a challenge I was convinced I wasn't up to. There really didn't seem to be a way out that would satisfy Kip without making me resentful. I went through it over and over again. Was there anything in sex that I liked? Or, maybe, even lower that bar—was there anything that I was at least neutral about—that I didn't feel either joy or displeasure with? And something not taxing?

Well, if there was anything in sex that I had fairly consistent good results in, it was fellatio. I think I'm pretty good at it—Kip wouldn't disagree. It gave Kip exquisite pleasure, which I also took pride in. I loved driving him crazy. Was it sexual for me? Yes and no. Sexual pride? Maybe. Sensual—in a way it let me enjoy sensuality while staying in control of how much sexual contact I wanted. But the prime benefit of oral sex was that, quite honestly, it involved my body the least. Others might disagree, and with good reason, but for me, oral sex was the simplest sex act that I could do, the one that stressed me the least and that would still bring the biggest payoff to Kip.

Kip was, as usual, in the bedroom. I knocked on the door, and he said to come in. He looked up from his book and said, "What?"

I bluntly said, "Maybe I could do oral sex."

He cocked his head to the side, carefully considering me. I knew what he was thinking: What was going on? Where did this come from? Whim? Desperation? Was I simply trying on another notion for size? I wasn't aware of how I'd toyed with Kip in the past every time that I brought up an idea to revive our sex life and then dropped it—for lack of interest. But I was pretty sure I could commit to oral sex. Kip didn't say anything. Probably not sure what he should say. It had come out of the blue.

Of course, as soon as the words came out of my mouth, I wondered if they were true. Here I am the crusader against unwanted sex, puzzling whether or not blow jobs count. One part of me says *nah*. Another part recalls that blow jobs can take a lot of effort. I remember the times that my jaw muscles throbbed with tension and I was in a position that was becoming more and more uncomfortable, but I froze there because I just *knew* Kip was near to climaxing. My hands would twist furiously, trying to find the right combo of movement that would send Kip over the edge.

Stunned by my own thoughts, I left the bedroom. Kip followed me out and waited for me to say something. Then he guardedly asked, "Are you sure you're okay with doing oral?"

The memory of the effort and the discomfort slipped in and out of my thoughts and I began feeling less brave about the whole thing. But then again, there were plenty of times that oral sex hadn't been a big deal. And sometimes even Kip had to stop me when he thought I was putting forth too much effort. So, what to do? There were just as many pros as cons. I began to debate myself: *Is it that big a deal? He's meeting you halfway, and besides, I'm the one who brought it up in the first place. Now it'll look like I'm reneging— again. Yet if I end up dreading sex all over again, no matter what type, what's the point?*

I left the living room and rambled into the kitchen. I opened and closed cupboards, peered inside the refrigerator, searched the freezer, looking for something comforting to eat. Nada.

But, then again, I thought, oral sex wasn't like that all the time and I had to come up with *something* that would be seen as a worthy movement in his direction because right now, sex was not even in the picture. However, because I'd taken a stalwart stance that women shouldn't compromise their bodies, I was still in a pickle. I needed to be totally straightforward. I didn't want to keep playing head games.

So I leaned over the counter and said from a solicitous distance, "*But . . .*" Crap, I didn't want to sound like I was taking anything back, but I needed to clarify my position to him as well as to myself. "But I still don't want to worry about your orgasms while giving you oral . . ." And then I decided that since I was so ickily uncomfortable now, I might as well go whole hog. "And I'm not going to deep-throat or swallow," I announced more arrogantly than I intended, like you do when you're really feeling trembly inside. So, to not make the declaration seem so abrupt, I explained, "If I didn't have to worry about that, it'd make doing oral sex a lot more neutral for me."

Kip put his feet up on the coffee table and leaned back, a look of consideration on his face. Then, after a couple minutes of silence, he replied, "Okay, I don't care about the deep-throating or swallowing." Then he paused. "And you don't have to keep at it until I orgasm."

"Really?" I was rather taken aback.

The interesting thing is that Kip had never insisted or even suggested I keep going until he reached orgasm. It was I who attacked the job like a sworn duty. Somehow I thought giving him great oral sex would distract him from the fact that *I* didn't enjoy much of the rest of sex very much. Well, gee. He'd noticed anyway. And steeling myself for the occasional challenges of oral sex made me put off and put off sex.

Kip repeated, "Are you sure you're okay with doing oral?"

"Yeah, as sure as I can be. I think it'll help a lot."

Now I had to really steel myself. Intercourse. Why not get the Big Kahuna out of the way? Feeling defensive again, I was waiting for an onslaught of arrows. Putting on my shining armor, I puffed out my chest and once again made a declaration: "If I don't want intercourse, I'm not going to do it." Intercourse, if it's unwanted, is really a slog. That's when I get really impatient and anxious. If I'm not into it, it's a bad deal.

"Okay," said Kip casually. "So, what about intercourse in particular don't you like?"

"Well, again, I don't want to worry about your orgasms." I paused for a beat, letting it sink in. "Because sometimes that requires a lot of effort. And that lands me back in the same spot. I mean the whole purpose here is to have sex that satisfies you, and that I'm not going to dread or resent. And sometimes, you know, it takes a while for you to get there, to the orgasm—that's going to exhaust me."

I didn't look at Kip for his reaction. I busied myself with making a cup of coffee, choosing a mug, reaching up for the sugar, getting the cream from the fridge. I wanted to give him a moment or two to privately react without me searching his face. I continued to sip my coffee, waiting—hoping—for him to come up with something I could live with and still respect myself. By the time I'd let go of the exaggerated interest in making a cup of joe, Kip was ready to talk. "You know, we don't have to keep going until orgasm with intercourse, either."

For the first time since I'd made my declaration, I looked directly at him.

"It's not like I don't know. I know I can sometimes take a long time," he said, "so why not just do it for a little while, then we can stop when you want to stop."

"All right," I replied, "but there are still going to be plenty of times I don't want intercourse at all. *Think* about it; could you really do without intercourse?"

Kip said, "I'll only have intercourse when you want it, too. If you don't, I'll settle for oral even if there's no climax."

"Really?"

"Really. And, if you give me intercourse instead of oral, you still don't have to worry if I come or not."

"Really?" I said again. That sounded like a pat answer. Just stop when I want? Maybe he didn't realize that left to my own devices, quittin' time could come mighty early. "How does that work? Because what if I stop before you want me to stop? You won't feel frustrated?"

"Not necessarily. You could do it like a kind of tease," he said. "We could make it fun—draw it out a little. That's my foreplay. I think that'll make it very exciting and unpredictable. I'd never know if I'm going to get full-on sex, oral, a sensual erotic massage, or whatever. I like not knowing. It'll be enough to get me going—or get me started. After that, I'll have enough for my imagination. I'll finish myself off. I could use porn or my image of you."

It's terrible, I'm so uncomfortable talking about masturbation, and I figured everyone else is. And even though Kip and I have talked about porn and masturbation before, I still tread shyly around it. I also felt kind of stupid about it, like I couldn't understand what for him was an obvious scenario. So, I was kind of apprehensive about asking him the details about how he'd finish himself off. Was this something we'd sort of do together, or what? I was trying to figure out the logistics. I asked, "Would I leave the bedroom?"

"Uh-huh. You would leave afterward, close the door behind you, and I'd have some privacy to continue at will." Kip was far more comfortable talking about masturbation than I was. His attitude was that just about everybody does it, so what's the big deal?

Besides that, he told me something I would never have thought of: he noted how men get off on viewing porn, whether in magazines, on TV, films, or the Internet. It's true. Men pour billions of dollars into a sex industry in which the majority of encounters are nonphysical. Is this only to tide over men who have no access to physical sex? Kip thought that yes, for most that's probably true. Yet it's also true that nonphysical sex represents a whole other realm of sexual titillation that men find very exciting on its own.

I stepped out of the kitchen, came into the living room with my coffee, and sat on the arm of the sofa. "Huh," I said. This was going better than I'd thought. It sounded like he already had it all thought out. And he wasn't mad and he wasn't pretending not to be mad. And I think I like what he's saying.

NO ORGASM REQUIRED

Maybe making the male orgasm optional would remove the mix of guilt and resentment that shadowed our sex lives. Most sexperts don't question the need for the male to orgasm. There have been exceptions to this rule, of course. In *The Better Sex Video Series,* one sexpert did say that the couple in question shouldn't worry about each other's orgasm—either his or hers. Kudos to this sexpert. But most of the sexperts I read seem to assume a man's orgasm is very important since men are the ones who really, really love sex. It's their thing. Unless there's a special circumstance, male orgasm has been a given. And that's what makes me not want to even begin anything, because if I lose interest right in the middle, I feel that I should keep marching on for him.

Now, seemingly, I was free to stop performing when I wanted, to put in as much or as little effort as I wanted into sex. The necessity of male orgasms would be thrown out. That solved most of my worries right there.

And what about my orgasm? Marcia and Lisa Douglass (and sometimes John Gray, depending on his mood) think that if women did have reliable orgasms, then they would be more likely to enjoy, and to desire, more sex. I'd already jettisoned that theory. Ironically, sex therapists like Gray and the Douglasses have made saying "okay, that's enough" even harder because *men* are also urged to keep going until their female partner comes. Such noble efforts on Kip's part (the twenty-minute tongue-numbing campout urged by Gray) only added to the guilt of reciprocity. I didn't want that kind of responsibility. I wanted to leave the party when I wanted to leave the party. When I couldn't, I felt backed into a corner.

So I added, "And I don't want you to worry about my orgasm, either, because I don't always reach the top of the mountain."

"Sounds fair to me," said Kip. "We won't worry about each other's orgasms. And if we're not sure if the other had one, it'll be the don't-ask, don't-tell policy."

DATE NIGHT

Then Kip dropped a big bomb: he thought that *he* should be the one to initiate sex. I took a noisy slurp of my coffee and started nervously swinging my leg back and forth. "If I left initiating sex to you, we'd never have sex," he said.

No argument there. Yet I hated to have that truth brought up, as bad as it was for Kip. Did he mean I wasn't supposed to have the option of turning him down? That would be a totally frightening and slave mentality. And I couldn't be at his sexual whim. That was just wrong. I'm not a lay-down Sally. But maybe I was taking him wrong. Kip couldn't possibly mean that. He's not a sexual bully.

"I don't get it. What do you mean, 'you'll be the initiator'?" I asked.

"Just what I said. I'll initiate sex. When I want sex, I'll let you know and—"

"*What?* I think you really need to explain this because I'm not getting it." I didn't like the sound of it. What's he pulling? Did he think that he was in the catbird seat and was now in a position to lay down the law? Must be. He was making the demands, holding our marriage hostage.

"You'll be in control of how long we'll have sex and what kind of sex we'll have," he quickly added. "One night could be just a striptease. No touching. Another could be an erotic massage, hand job, or oral sex. Or another night we could have intercourse if *you* were in the mood. Or some sort of combination of those. That would be entirely in your control."

Hmm. True. But I was still trying to think if this was a fair trade-off. Yeah, I remember Lister saying something like this, but I quickly dismissed it:

> It may be a quickie. It may be a hand job. It may mean oral sex, one way only. The point is for you two to find a way to satisfy him without taxing you too much. Sometimes it's not the idea of sex per se you object to but the prospect of what's involved. You don't have the energy or interest for a full production: trying to get aroused, trying to stay aroused, trying to reach orgasm, waiting for him to reach orgasm.

I think I dismissed what Lister said here because of the context. The passage was couched in a section on suffering a low libido phase during the stage of having a young family. Giving some kind of sex was suggested as a temporary solution to a problem that would eventually go away, but I deemed my low libido to be part of my nature, not my circumstance. Not to mention that much of her book seems aimed at attending to male sexuality. So I put Lister more on a par with Gray's mandatory giving-in. But after hearing what Kip had to say, especially since he hadn't read a word of Lister, I thought, why not? Maybe Lister meant it as a temporary stop-gap, but what's temporary? Her prescription for the "family stage" of life might easily run a few years. Couldn't it be effective before kids, after kids, or for folks with no kids?

"You see how it works?" he asked.

"Yeah, but I don't know if I'll like you just springing sex on me."

I was starting to think of any number of sexperts who advised me to be sexually spontaneous, accessible, and gift-giving at the drop of a hat. And not my hat.

Kip paced around the living room, stroking his chin—a move I was sure he had stolen from me, which I stole from episodes of *Matlock*. I crossed my arms and watched him walk around. I think there's going to be a stalemate.

Kip turned to face me with an exaggerated look of contemplation, something he does from time to time to infuse a little humor into contentious matters. "Why don't we set up certain days for sex? Then it won't take you by surprise."

I remembered shows and articles that said a couple should plan sex—date nights—so that they wouldn't keep putting it off. And knowing myself, that was probably a good idea. Seen this way, the idea that Kip determined when those days would be didn't seem as chauvinistic as I had first thought.

"All right," I said. I didn't want to sound all caught up in dread this soon out of the gate, but I needed specifics. Like how many times a week we're talking about here. I said casually, "So, um, what days were you thinking about?"

"Three days, that sounds about right."

"Huh." Knot in stomach.

Kip stood there looking at me. I said "huh" again. I slowly nodded and pressed my lips tightly together as if I was considering his idea even though I could barely keep my eyes from bulging out of my head. Kip kept looking to me to give a more decisive answer. When I said "huh" for a fourth time, he intuited that I was having a hard time swallowing three nights of sex per week.

"Just some kind of sexual stimulation a couple of those nights and maybe on the weekend something, you know, more"—he was struggling for the right word—". . . elaborate." I didn't know if that was any different from "gourmet sex." I kind of hoped it was different.

"Okay, that's an idea," I said, and then sat down and turned on the national news.

I concentrated on Brian Williams's tie. It had a sheen on it that made it change colors when he moved. I didn't want to think about anything else but that tie. I knew that Kip was probably anxious for me to settle things, but I wasn't ready yet. For some reason, I desperately wanted a peanut-butter-and-jelly sandwich.

I knew I had to shift my focus back to the topic at hand. I physically shifted the position of my legs on the table to get the process started. I remembered years of going back and forth with on-again, off-again sex. Kip was fed up with the push and pull. He was fed up with trying to get me in the mood. Fed up with me coming out of the bathroom looking anxious and complaining because my hair was wrong and the lingerie didn't fit right. Truth to tell, I still didn't trust this plan of Kip's and thought it was going to crash and burn immediately after takeoff. We'd be left with another sexual disappointment in our marriage. Another scar. Despite this worry, I agreed to try it.

My part was simple: at least visually stimulate him. And stop when I wanted to stop. Don't go beyond what is comfortable to me. There were certain conditions: He would initiate on three pre-arranged nights a week. On two of those nights I didn't have to give him anything more than a visual show if I didn't want to do more than that. One night a week I would include genital stimulation: blow job, hand job, that sort of thing; it could, but need not, involve intercourse. So, we agreed on three nights a week that would work for both of us, and tried out the new arrangement.

Twenty-three

THE COMPROMISE

In the end, I found that love does not conquer all—it does not conquer hunger and it won't conquer sex. I can't tell you how mad and sad that made me. I didn't want to believe that sex could take up so much room in a marriage.

But sex is hardwired in. So, if the two of you can't come to terms on the contents of a sex agreement, then you're unlikely to have a happy marriage. Instead, if you're a woman, grab a bottle of wine, pour yourself a big glass, and watch *Bridget Jones's Diary* over and over again. If you're a guy, go down to Slack Sally's, get a stiff drink, and wonder why all women can't be as easy with their sexuality as the pole dancers.

To my amusement, even *FHM* and *Complete Woman* had McNugget articles recommending sex contracts. I wasn't the only one to conclude that a couple should have a concrete understanding of sexual expectations. At first, I thought the idea of negotiating a sex agreement was funny, in a cynical sort of way. Like Cinderella being run over by her own pumpkin carriage.

But underneath all my protective layers, the idea of a sex agreement was basically frightening. Because it didn't give me any mental wiggle room. I had to face myself. Who was I sexually? I believe that many women asking themselves the same question would find that who we are sexually has little in common with who men are sexually, or who we've been pretending to be. The frightening part is that if we stick up for our own sexuality, we're scared we're going to lose any chance of getting a man or keeping him. Maybe so. Nonetheless, I thought I owed Kip honesty. It's men and women's moral obligation to be honest with one another before binding themselves together in a lifelong commitment—no matter what the consequences. Obviously, I didn't do that until way after we were married and Kip was also naive enough to hold on to our relationship by sharing in the delusion.

When we force ourselves to become specific and detail our expectations in relation to another person, we are also allowing *them* to make more realistic choices, giving everyone a better shot at future happiness. And that's all any of us can do—give it a shot, but we owe it to one another to give it our best shot.

Of course, actually signing a legally binding *sexual* agreement is another story. I'm sure it can be done and undoubtedly is already included in the contents of more general prenuptial agreements. But I sure don't advise people to do this. Quite frankly, it's not in the best interest of the nation to have our civil courts clogged with the embarrassing minutiae of our unfortunate sex lives. Second, there are just some things that a couple needs to work out between themselves on an entirely personal and private level. The point is to save yourselves years of conflict.

PRACTICE MAKES PERFECT

My agreement with Kip went like this: There were times when I'd give him little or no genital stimulation. I'd dress in fancy lingerie and give him a hot strip dance. We had a couple of provisos: The less genital stimulation I gave him or genital access I allowed him, the more I would step up on the visuals. Thus if I felt jeans-and-a-shirt-day, I'd give him some oral action. If I didn't want to get involved with anyone's genitals, including my own, then it was all about being eye candy. I wanted to keep it light and fun for myself. I thought, *What makes it easy and fun for me?* The closer I could get to that personal ideal (short of completely replacing sex with chocolate), the happier we'd both be.

Before, lingerie had been my sexual crutch. That was because a look, the perfect look, had to substitute and compensate for my lack of sexual appetite. The look had to carry me through the sex act itself. I thought if I looked sexy, it would make me magically feel horny.

In the bedroom, I tried to be a woman with a capital *W*. But as I'd put on my lipstick, I'd avoid looking at the rest of my face in the mirror. I was trying to stave off what inevitably happens. I'd start seeing things. Imperfections. My thigh-high stockings were creeping down. I'd put too much hairspray in my hair and now it looked weird. I'd think my bustier was oddly bisecting my breasts. I'd tussle frantically with my boobs, pushing them up, pushing them to the center, pushing them down. Well, who the hell cares anyway since my hair is lying on my head like chunks of concrete?

In sitcoms and movies, when a woman comes out of the bath-room in lingerie, it means she's horny and looking to get sex. So lin-gerie became my front, my fake-out. Deep down I knew I wasn't feeling as sexual as my lingerie and makeup were letting on. But the image of lust was all I had. Now it is what it is—lingerie. I could finally relax and enjoy looking hot because I no longer had to live up to some promise I thought my outfits were making. I could take vain pleasure in Kip's appreciation without having to deliver.

When it came to actually performing sex acts themselves, whether a sensual massage or oral sex, I was curious to see how our new arrangement would play itself out in our own little reality show. Of course I was unsure of myself initially, and I expressed that doubt by trying a bit too hard at first, but in subsequent episodes, I learned to let my feelings guide how much and how long.

For instance, instead of going all-out and taking the whole thing in my mouth for a session I hoped would end in his mind-blowing orgasm, I merely teased his penis with my tongue. I stopped when I wanted to. If I felt like quitting after a couple of minutes, that's ex-actly what I did.

Having a positive attitude toward sex was key to my success. I don't mean thinking myself into a positive attitude. And I definitely don't mean thinking sexy thoughts. I mean that when sex was no longer a chore, I could approach it positively, without dread. I liked not having to keep reminding myself of the wonderful gift I was giv-ing my husband. I didn't want to be psyching myself up for sex. Now, that doesn't mean that I greet sexual episodes like a ticket to a carnival. No, to the contrary, this plan was designed for those very days when I'm the most apathetic about sex (remember, that's what got this whole thing started). It's during those times that I could consult my mental menu of sex and decide on something that's the most effortless or least time-consuming.

And I could go into it with confidence because I knew I was not getting myself into anything other than what I wanted to do and for how long I wanted to do it. But I still had to show up.

COMFORTABLE OUTCOME

Possibly the most important thing that makes the agreement work is that my comfort is never optional. I don't do anything I'm not comfortable with. Ever since I hit adolescence, I've felt pressure from the media, the sexperts, and boyfriends to push past my so-called inhibitions, or in today's parlance, boundaries and zones. Most of my sexual encounters were filled with the fear that I was expected to do more than I wanted to. Or that I had to progress into "naughtier" territory. I think it's a mistake to take the concept of challenging yourself and apply it to sex. Overall, it doesn't fit very well.

For instance, I pushed past my fear when I learned to swim, when I took a statistics class, when I gave speeches in front of audiences. Pushing past boundaries can give you strength and build your character. But with sex, it's usually letting a man push into women's boundaries—usually for his pleasure, as it often turns out, not the woman's. Perhaps that's because it's usually men who are taking our measure. They provide the yardstick for how far women should jump. Even though much, if not most, sex advice we get is from women, it's based upon the sexual happiness of men. Usually, men don't have to push past their boundaries to try something kinky or new. If there is any pushing to be done, it's to get their

partner to try it. All these stretch-yourself, try-anything-once rec-
ommendations were spun as if they were something women wanted
for themselves but just didn't know it.

My ground rule is this: I don't do anything I think will be uncomfortable mentally or physically. So it's either got to be something I like doing or that I'm at least neutral about. There are some
things I know I won't do. Like have anal sex. I'm not going to emu-
late what *Penthouse* churns out.

I realize that my sexual preferences aren't exactly logical. Some
of the reasons I have for not liking cunnilingus could also apply to
fellatio, which I don't mind. But I want to show you that some of
our sexual preferences and quirks don't make sense—and they
don't have to. If I don't want to do a particular sex act, I don't do it.
I needn't defend my choice.

Working out a sex agreement that respected my needs and preferences left me feeling at ease, confident, and in control of what I
wanted to happen sexually. It provided a relief so great that I finally
felt I could trust myself again. I knew that I wasn't playing mind
games or talking myself into things, or talking myself out. More often than not, I end up feeling pretty smug after a sex session. That
smugness comes from knowing I'm able to sexually satisfy Kip
without compromising myself. In that way, I can actually enjoy being sexual for him as long as it's my way.

Satisfaction is, of course, defined differently in my marriage.
Orgasm is still important to Kip, but that doesn't mean I have to
keep trying to physically stimulate him until he has one. If he has
an orgasm during our time together, fine. If not, I just need to provide enough sexual stimulation (sometimes visual, sometimes genital, sometimes both) so that he can bring himself to orgasm later if
he wants.

ROMANCING

Ideally, sexual pleasure would be mutual—it would make things much simpler. But most of the time for me, that isn't the case. So what do I get out of all this?

Gray, Love, and Lister say that if you keep your man sexually happy, you'll reap the benefits as a by-product. He'll be nicer, more romantic, etc. Though I think their motives are suspect—a vague assurance meant as an intangible carrot goading women into unwanted sex—I have to admit they have a point. But while they urge women to have unwanted sex on men's terms, I think that having sex that *doesn't* compromise a woman is enough to bring about those rewards.

Kip even encouraged me to think of something concrete that would make me feel special in return for giving him sexual pleasure. We go out a lot more than we used to, we socialize more, have a few nights on the town. Though I'm the one who usually "initiates" this, Kip no longer drags his feet about coming along. One of my favorite things is to go out to coffee houses with fireplaces and soft chairs, sipping whatever, chatting, watching people, playing an occasional game of chess. Kip is more of a homebody. For the most part, he sees no advantage in going out for coffee when I've got it right here. But take me out he did. It was a sea change. And after a while he began to take turns suggesting we go out for walks, or dinner, or a leisurely read with a Sunday paper over coffee and muffins at a cozy little coffee place. And that puts me in a happier, confident, more loving mood.

I still fall short of thinking that sex is a spiritual experience for men, but it does seem that the contract at least took away his simmering resentment that I had no interest in him sexually and that his needs weren't going to be met. When we found a way where we could engage in sexual activities that satisfied him without causing resentment in me, a cloud lifted from our marriage. Kip's whole demeanor toward me changed. I'm abashed to say that many of the sexperts I criticized were right on this: Kip became a more loving, attentive, and communicative man. Our marriage became more intimate in other areas. He became more affectionate, happier. I watched this change slowly take place. To me, it was impossible to fathom that sex could make such a difference. But it did.

It turns out that the changes I saw in Kip *were* enough of a reward for me. I loved it. Not only that, another very surprising reward for me is that I ended up feeling more feminine. Normally, I didn't give a hoot about feeling feminine or pampered or any such thing. But I liked the lingerie and sexy outfits. Now that they no longer meant a night of sex I was sure to resent, I was free to enjoy being a *femme* as just another aspect of myself. It made me feel more sensual in a sexual sense, but as far as lustful, if anything, the effect was indirect—an "ain't I sexy and know it" kind of thing. And I know the difference between feeling sexy and feeling lustful. That was just fine with my husband because my looking sexy translated into visual teasing, which he loves, and a little this and a little that—which I determined. It was very freeing and very fun.

MORPHING THE DETAILS

After a year, Kip wanted to change our agreement, which had already morphed several times in small ways. And that's to be expected. But now Kip wanted to test the waters in a bigger way. He mentioned he'd like a more active role in the timing of sex. Instead of me determining the pace, he wanted to do it. The content of the sex would still be left to me. Well, sort of. He said he'd like to have a little more control over the physical contact, too.

I said, "Let me think about this."

I didn't know what to say, I liked our arrangement. He initiated on certain nights, but I liked being in control of the pace and the content of sex. That was just fine with me and I didn't really want to play with it. But I at least had to hear Kip out, even though I was sure I wasn't going to like what he had to say.

"It's nothing really big. Nothing, I don't know, I *need* to do."

"Well, c'mon. Just tell me." *Or don't, and I can live in peace forever.*

"I was thinking that I could determine the pace of the sex."

"What?"

"During sex, what happens is completely on your terms—and when it happens."

I nod my head. That's why it works.

"I know you like to be in control," he said.

"No, you're making it sound like I like to be in control of you. That's not it. I just want to be in control over what happens during sex. There's a difference." I was frustrated by my own inability to get the finer aspects of my point across. "Don't make this into a personal power issue."

"I know that. I already know that, so calm down," he said, motioning the palms of his hands to the floor. "It's not a big thing. Forget I brought it up."

"No. Don't pull that passive-aggressive crap with me. Let's discuss it, okay? My head's not going to explode. Really. So what were you thinking?" I asked.

"Well, maybe we could do it something like this: I would be

more involved in the pacing of the sex, instead of you always calling the shots about when. You know, sometimes you just stop, walk out into the living room, get a Coke or whatever, and then come back in."

"Yeah, well, that's the point. I could stop and start when I wanted. You said you liked the unpredictability of it."

"I did. But now I'd like to be a more, ya know, a more active participant." Then Kip firmed up that rather politic answer. "I'd like to be the one calling the shots, too. I'd like to ring the bell and have you come in when I want or leave and I can masturbate, and then motion to you to come in again."

Hmm. "What about the sex itself? Not just the timing of the sex acts. You already determine the days—I mean, I only do what I want to do, right? So if I want you to touch me, you can touch me. If I want to give you oral, or if I want intercourse, I'm the one in charge of that. Is that what you don't like, too? Does it—does it make you feel too passive or something?" Kip ruffled his hair. I could see he didn't know how to answer.

"Yeah, in a way, I'm a little tired of waiting for your signals. I like to be more actively involved in my pleasure, too."

"We could try it that way. I don't know."

"Like I said, I understand. And if it's going to make you less comfortable and sexual, forget it. Really."

Did he mean that, or was he just placating me?

I wasn't in the mood to cook a meal and I wasn't in the mood for a frozen pizza. In fact, I wasn't in the mood to be at home period. I needed a place to decompress. "Let's go somewhere," I said.

"Where?"

"I don't know, just let's go somewhere."

"To eat or do you want to get coffee?"

"I don't know, are you hungry?"

"I could eat. Do you want to go to the Charlestown?"

"Yeah, sounds good." I knew we would probably end up at the Charlestown from the get-go—it's about as close to a diner as West Seattle can get. I didn't mind going there, kind of liked the place, but I still liked the charade that we'd actually go somewhere else. The truth is, the food's not the best, but it's familiar, cheap, and local. We grab a table and I pretend to look over the menu. I know I'm getting a mocha shake. Kip'll get the mushroom burger and a side of spicy, curly fries, which I'll share. First, I need real coffee. A young man with bristly hair and a pencil tucked behind his ear takes our order. I get my coffee in less than a nanosecond. I love that about the Charlestown. Kip slides the sugar caddy over to me. It's a comforting ritual; pouring the sugar onto my spoon, hearing the ting, ting as I stir it in, adding the cream slowly until I get a light caramel swirl. How long have we been coming here? And why couldn't I let go of my suspicions? My fear that being a sexual failure will kill us eventually.

My milk shake comes, but I don't feel like drinking it. I pout. "But what if it doesn't work for us?"

In exasperation, Kip says, "Stop anticipating the worst!" He leans forward and says in a hushed voice, "Look at it this way, it's a start. I don't know how else to prove I'm in this with you."

"Yeah, I suppose." Kip's meal comes and I lean back as the waiter refills my coffee. Kip smacks the bottom of the bottle of ketchup, but it won't budge. He resorts to taking a butter knife and sticking it into the mouth to counteract whatever other law of physics is impeding the force of gravity. The ketchup glug-glugs onto the plate.

Could I handle this new change to our sexual agreement? Kip

said I didn't have to. But was it possible for me? What amount of control could I give up and still feel comfortable *and* uncompromised? I asked Kip, "How much do you need to feel more active in our sex sessions?"

Kip sighed. "It sounds like you're not going to be into it."

"Well, the truth is, I'm probably not. I'm going to feel that sex is out of my hands again." I looked at him. "So what do we do?"

"Okay, how about this? You step up the visuals. More outfits, and be a lot higher maintenance, every day."

He'd asked that as part of our previous agreement. And I always promise I'll do that. But I keep ending up in my black, bagged-out jeans and some generic top. My hair remains the same as when I fell out of bed. And during the cold, wet, Seattle winters, I tend to diet but not exercise. My butt is beginning to look like two sacks of cottage cheese. Kip's not being chauvinistic. I'm the one who complains about my butt. But since I'm complaining about it, he figures I might as well do something about it.

"But don't think you've got to be in perfect shape. Look at me," he says, pulling up his shirt and squeezing his belly. "Flab." So, though we're both pretty slender, it was time to put some muscle into our physiques. But it was understood it would be a bigger give on my side. Because Kip had conceded a good deal to my sexual comfort and limits, he wanted in exchange more effort put forth on my part in the visual department, not just in bed, but every day.

Oh, he said, by the way, would I consider lap dances?

"Well, I've never given one before." Coincidentally, at this time, Seattle was considering a ban on lap dances in strip clubs. (But the private rooms remain; what goes on behind the curtains, huh? Tea, scones, and polite conversation?) I shake my head to clear the nasty little pictures I had out of my mind so I could stop obsessing about strip clubs. But too late, I'm at it again. "How do *you* know what a lap dance is?"

"Of course, c'mon, who doesn't?"

Well, I've never done one but I got a good idea from the movie *Women Versus Men*.

We watched *Women Versus Men* together. In one scene, a woman had followed her husband and her friend's husband to a "strip" joint. She sneaked in through the back and saw that much more than stripping was going on; it was beating music, pole dancing, *and* fully naked women sitting in the lap of her husband and his friend, grinding on them as they buried their faces in the women's bare breasts. In a sickened state of shock, she ran back out to the parking lot and called her friend on her cell phone. She told her, "You'd never believe where they're at. A strip club." Her friend, a psychologist, told her to calm down. The guys were just blowing off steam watching women dance. The wife in the parking lot said no, that most definitely was not all. It was like Sodom and Gomorrah in there! So lap dances didn't have good associations for me. I'd have to think about it.

In a nutshell, this was the compromise. I could still be in control. But in exchange, I'd make more of an effort to look sexy every day, even when (especially when) he'd be the only one who saw me. It was important to Kip because the daily effort represented my bowing to his pleasure. I was conceding to his wishes enough to put energy, time, and work into expressly pleasing him.

I realized that it was kind of a power thing. He needed, to feel respected and yes, manly in our sexual relationship. I needed to feel in control of what happened during a session of sex. There were other little things we worked out along the way. If I *did* give him a lap dance, he wanted the opportunity to grope me—like my breasts. But I balked at that. I didn't want unwanted groping. So the choice was either I *wouldn't* do a lap dance *unless* I wanted to be freely touched by him. Or, I could give him a lap dance on the condition that he *could* touch me, but only when I wanted him to, and I'd have a prearranged signal for him to stand down, and he'd stop, and I could continue with the lap dance. I liked this because I got to let loose the exhibitionist and tease within me, without having to pay up at the end.

When I was free to do what I wanted, my sexuality took me by surprise. It is not necessarily expressed in orgasms or a desire for physical stimulation. And I won't say that having the pressure off my sexual performance resulted in more lust or more orgasms. It hasn't. Instead, much to my surprise (and old-school feminist dismay), my sexuality is largely the pleasure of being seen and admired as a sexual creature.

As for Kip, he may not get a lot of what he wants. But he gets sex more regularly, more confidently, and without my dodging or procrastinating. And he can sense that. Thus he can be more confident that I don't approach sex with dread but as an opportunity to please him without compromising myself. If I begin to enjoy a particular episode, which I now often do, that's a bonus for me and him. And by enjoyment, I don't mean climaxing.

Some nights I put more effort into it than others, depending on my mood. It's gratifying when he goes crazy. And I like having intercourse with Kip on occasion. I like the feeling of him inside me. But I would be lying to say that I give him direct genital stimulation only when I feel like it. There are times I think, *He deserves this*. Yet it isn't gift-giving in the sexpert sense. I don't grin and bear it. I don't do it on a consistent basis. It's not a duty. Whatever I do grows out of the moment, out of a genuine impulse. I might be moved by playfulness, or gratitude, or because I'm enjoying my effect on him. My compass point is always my own comfort and self-respect—not love.

Giving sex out of love is a slippery slope. The old "If you love him you would . . ." breeds guilt and resentment. I think it's that simple. So I give only sex I'm comfortable with. Sex is to fulfill my husband's needs and that maintains a happier marriage and that's what opens the door for love. Now that there is less tension in our relationship, we love each other more than ever.

But the love must go both ways. I can't have him love me while I resent him. What's the use of that? That is what the sexperts never considered, and that is why it is so important that sex he on my terms.

*B*ut it wasn't all a fairy tale. Though Kip was quite happy with this turn of events, it didn't mean that our life magically turned into *The Sound of Music* (before they were chased by the Nazis). I found that having sex on a regular basis isn't a guarantee of fidelity. Men drift for a whole lot of other reasons. They can be happy with their sex lives and still find a reason to become fascinated with another woman. I didn't know that. Even Mo'nique, for whatever reason, got divorced. I had bought the line that men just needed wild sex with their mates to be happily devoted. Boy, was I wrong. And I didn't find this out from any self-help book. I had ten blue-cat-fits when Kip nicely illustrated my point.

Twenty-four

PEACHES AND CREAM

Just recently, we went to Amour, a lovers' boutique. We were shopping for sexy clothing and lingerie. Nothing fluffy. All shiny vinyl, baby. Pure streetwalker clothes. And not the twenty-buck hookers that give blow jobs in an alley. I mean the seventy-five-dollar pros with their own seedy hotel room and pimp. Yup, I was a class act.

Okay, so there I was, all done up like a woman of ill repute. Nasty girl. Doing nasty things. And then . . .

A couple of weeks later, a new neighbor was in the process of moving into our apartment building. Howdy, neighbor! When we first met her, she was wearing a cotton, flower-print dress that hung midcalf, with plain flats. Her hair was a simple brown ponytail. She wore little makeup, if any at all, and had a peaches-and-cream

complexion. Pretty, but not beautiful, she seemed to have a mag-
netic effect on Kip. He was falling all over himself asking if she
needed help moving her furniture in. There are two odd things
about this. First, Kip absolutely hates moving furniture—for anybody. Jesus Christ himself could come down and ask Kip to move a
Barcalounger and he would say, "Oops, gotta get my hair cut." Second, she already had a boyfriend, who, she said, was right on his
way to help her. While he had yet to show up, Kip kept asking her if
there was anything, anything at all, he could do to help. The thing
is that Kip never flirts, at least not around me; he's too shy or careful. Now he'd lost complete control and flirted right in my face. He
was practically carrying her over the threshold.

Oh, I was ticked. When he kept asking me after she had moved
in if I thought the boyfriend was living with her full-time or not, I
blew up. Here I was, masturbating in front of my husband in a
miniskirt and black vinyl boots and he wanted to get it on with a
woman who looked like she came straight out of the youth ministry.
What in the Pope's hat was this about?

I have a sixth sense when it comes to Kip's interest in someone
else. My guilt for not being a more libidinous woman bubbles up
everywhere. When I'm with Kip, grocery shopping can be a mine-
field. Women wearing "Juicy Couture" on their butts stroll up and
down the aisle. Women not wearing enough material to have room
for the Juicy Couture inscription stand in line with teensy little
skirts or peeking thongs and bulging tops, long, shiny hair, and . . .
oh God, I'm making myself sick. We always seem to get caught in a
long line behind them, and I'm watching my husband trying not to
let on he's watching them. But *this* girl, judging by her well-
scrubbed, chaste look, would never be a blip on my radar.

I confronted him. "How could you do this to me? How?" It

seemed like I was a double-coupon whore next to Miss Peaches and Cream. Could Kip flip on me that fast?

Kip said, "It's not what you think . . . I was just helping . . . and just curious if her boyfriend was, you know, really her boyfriend or friend. It's . . . curiosity."

"Look. I know you. I know you don't take an interest in the neighbors. None. I'm not stupid."

He said she seemed very nice. A sweet person. And he admitted, yes, he was "sort of" attracted to her.

I turned to him, one hand on my hip. "How'd you suddenly get attracted to a girl who fell off the milk truck while you're encouraging me to trick out as a slut?" God, I felt like a used condom.

"I don't know. I honestly don't."

"You don't? You *don't*?" Worse yet, it sure looked like a *romantic* attraction.

"Joan . . ."

"Bull!"

I cannot believe this. I don't need this crap. I DO NOT NEED THIS. I shouldered past him and headed out the door.

After angrily leaving Kip behind in the apartment, I went to a place I go to whenever I'm feeling really happy about something or really bad—a small tract of land behind a dead-end street that looks out over the water. At night, the brilliant lights of downtown Seattle reflect in the water, making another glittering city waving on its surface. The strong night wind blows away my anger, then the self-pity lying underneath, then the sadness that rests beneath that. I'm stripped to the bare bones.

I stand there ten, fifteen, twenty minutes, gathering strength. Then I hear Kip's voice behind me. "Hey, hey." He puts a hand on my shoulder.

"Hey, hey *what?*" I'm irritated by the interruption. It weakens me.

"It's okay."

"No, it isn't."

"You're blowing this . . ." Then he hesitates. He knows I hate it when he says that. "We're okay." Silence. "We're okay. You and me, we're okay."

Right.

"We're not okay. Do you understand? We're not. You flipped on me. You flipped on me like that!" I said, snapping my fingers. "What's next? Dame Edna? Let's make the conversation shorter—is there any type of woman out there you wouldn't heave a sofa for? Because I sure as hell can't get you to pull a chair out for me." Kip looked at me with astonishment. "Well?" I said to his silence. "Am I too cheap and easy for you now?" Even under the dimness of the streetlight, I could see Kip's face harden. I could tell he was outraged by the crudeness of my question and what it suggested.

Now Kip was standing there, his face taught with frustration—maybe even resentment. He was taking slow, deep breaths. I registered all this and took the opportunity to prick at the balloon: I asked him if he had to do it all over again, would he have gotten married? There was a pause so long that I could have knitted little caps and cardigans for every team in the NFL, planned a Toys for Tots charity gala, and still had time to engage Martha Stewart on plant-care tips most favorable for Boston ferns.

Finally, he said, "I've already slogged through it this far." Slogged? Slogged! "I tell you what, I'd never get married again." Ouchy, ouchy, ouch. I had backed into the thornbush that I myself had planted.

"Well, that's a ringing endorsement for marriage."

"I'm going."

I turned to watch him disappear around the corner. Then turned back around and stared at the city.

When Kip married me, he had not had a lot of experience with women. He thought I was going to be a lot more even-tempered, sexy, confident, and fun than I actually was. I was older and had been around the block two or ten times. I tried to warn him, at least I can say that much for myself. I thought he was the sweetest, kindest, and most attentive guy I'd ever gone out with. And he thought I was sophisticated and funny. Little did we know how lust and love would change us over time.

Because of my past experience with crummy relationships, I had simmering doubts about whether men and women could truly love one another in a stable relationship; we're so different in so many ways. Now my doubts boiled over. I walked back down the dark streets until I got to the intersection of College and California. A couple was coming out of Yen Wor's, a happy little dinner date, I'm sure. I said under my breath, "You'll regret it." I must have said it louder than I intended because the woman looked straight at me. That's right. Crazy lady over here. I wished I were a crazy lady. Then I could speak my mind to anyone: "Hello, you look like a fine young couple. But you'll just end up breaking up, or worse, hanging on for no good reason. Sorry to bring bad tidings. Good night and have a pleasant evening." I wanted to be Mary Poppins and spout things like "Romance is tomfoolery!" I'd appear magically in churches in the heartland and warn couples away from the altar with the insistent tap of my umbrella. Then I'd prissily adjust my hat and fly to the vast nuptial sands of Vegas, where I'm sorely needed.

My daydream was ended by an unfortunate step into the mush of a discarded burger. By the time I got home, Kip had a hazelnut cappuccino waiting for me. He had left in frustration but now greeted me with a peace offering. I was touched by his thoughtfulness but wasn't ready to give up the argument, the conversation, the whatever it was we were having. Kip saw this in my face and quietly sighed, setting the coffee cup on the table and rubbing the back of his neck in anticipation of a muscle cramp.

"You were attracted to her."

"Yeah."

"Sexually attracted."

"I didn't get a *boner*. But yeah, I was sexually attracted."

"Romantic, too?" I already knew the answer, but I wondered if he'd fess up.

"Yes, romantically attracted, too." I was crestfallen by the readiness of his answers. Deep down I wanted a denial. But Kip didn't even pause.

"Why? We were doing so well. What *moved* you to become so infatuated?" I hated the plaintive sound of my voice.

Kip said in a low, barely perceptible voice, "I don't know."

"Do you know why you married me?" He put up his hand in fatigued dismissal. I said loudly, "I don't want to be humiliated by your thoughtless infatuations—sexual, romantic, whatever." I was about to say more, but I no longer had the energy to continue our sorry rendition of *Who's Afraid of Virginia Woolf?* I could see he was angered and disappointed by my stubbornly jaundiced view of love.

With surprisingly adamant emotion Kip said that even though he might very well like the idea of more than one sex partner, or one kind of sex partner, he also valued the love and intimacy of a woman. "I want affection, too," he said. Kip added softly, "I want a companion who can laugh, commiserate, and have cutenesses with me" (his word for getting all lovey-dovey and cuddly). I put my head down and stared at my feet, not sure how I should react.

Much later I realized Kip was telling the truth. He *didn't* know why he was so enamored with her. He wasn't dissing me. I didn't understand it at the time, but while Kip and many men might have a favorite type, like busty, young, and long-legged, until they look identical to one another (besides being blond, brunette, or red-headed), they can also be attracted to other types as well. Kip is also attracted to the small-breasted, snooty Paris Hilton, me, naughty secretaries, and, apparently, the guileless meadow flower. It took a while before I understood that the romantic preferences of all of us can take us by surprise. Men can't always anticipate what kind of woman is going to knock them in the stomach, the kind of woman who will drive them to move furniture.

Even after we worked out our sex life, Kip's sexual and romantic inclinations persisted. I spent years stubbornly trying to find some formula that would make for a perfectly monogamous and happy marriage. But there wasn't any magic or even reliable formula. Could be he's angry at me, could be he's frustrated by his job, could be he had fantasies he didn't want me to know about. I understood that I was not privy to what went on in Kip's mind. Maybe it doesn't matter what I do. Maybe he'll just get terribly irritated with me one night for browbeating Paris or stealing the last Coke. Could just be novelty and temptation in a man's world of gentlemen's clubs and those pesky CAKE feminists with parties that put Spring Break's lewd revelry to shame. Maybe just the daily distraction of pretty young women he sees will translate into attraction that has nothing to do with me. To some degree I can understand. I've had a completely capricious attraction to a man that went against type.

For instance, I usually like the dangerous-looking guys, tall men with five-o'-clock shadow, nice lips, and wide shoulders. Or the off-beat types, with long hair, dark glasses, tight jeans, earrings, and boots. But one time I was walking quickly beside the tall buildings in downtown Cleveland. I had a briefcase full of papers that had to get to the United Way building. I took a shortcut up Ninth, past a loading dock. Just as I was about to turn down another side street, I saw a man crossing diagonally. He was an ordinary-looking, unre-markable man. Maybe about five-eight. He wore a white T-shirt and jeans. He had straight brown hair in a conventional tapered cut just above his neck. It was blowing ever so slightly back from his face be-cause he was also hustling somewhere. There was something about him that made me want to speak to him. I stopped in my tracks and watched him walk on, intensely wistful. What would, what *could*, I have said to him? For some unknown reason, he struck me as quick-witted and thoughtful. The man I missed who could've been my true soul mate, not Kip.

These romantic mirages can come from anywhere. I never told Kip about it. Nearly five years later and I still remember him. As a sexual fantasy? No. And it's a rarity that I even think about him at all now. But when I do, the picture is crystal clear. Still, I know men are far more likely than women to feel the desire for sexual freedom and to act on it. That's why there's a huge sex industry, strip clubs, and prostitutes. And that's why their fantasies are all the more upsetting and threatening.

I sipped on my cappuccino and then swirled it around in fake nonchalance. A car blasted its horn. I glanced toward the window, but the reflection of the lamp made it impossible to see outside. I said, "No more subconscious stuff. I just want to know that *you* know what you're doing."

"I do now . . . and I'm sorry."

"Okay." I was glad to hear the wisp of sorrow in his voice. Aside from all the drama, of course I knew he loved me. And no denying it, I loved him, too. Had I blown this out of proportion?

I leaned an elbow on the table and rested my head on my knuckles. I desperately wanted to wring an intellectual, rational understanding from this night, to trump our messy humanity, to overcome it.

I turned my eyes to Kip. "Because we can observe it, does that mean we're above it?"

"I think insight helps. Or maybe we're all in it up to our necks." He looked tired. "Drink your cappuccino and let's get some sleep."

I sat at the kitchen table, munching on a brownie while Kip was getting ready for bed. Considering seemingly intractable problems was always easier with chocolate at hand. The storm had passed, but I still found the unpredictable sexual and romantic preferences of my husband plenty disturbing. Men are very promiscuous by nature, some in body and some in spirit. Luckily for me, Kip's philandered only in his imagination. As I took another bite of the brownie, I had an epiphany. There *was* a beneficial side effect that came out of this morass of jealousy, fantasy, and doubt. I realized that if my husband became attracted to someone else, it certainly needn't be because he was not getting enough hot sex from his wife. And that takes a lot of blame off of me. There will always be mirages, no matter what, but at least now we both understood the difference between a mirage and who we really do know and why we value them. And I could only hope that mattered.

Kip came out of the bathroom in his flannel robe, and saw that I hadn't changed into my jammies. He bent down to give me a warm hug. "Are you going to stay up all night going over and over this?"

"Well, maybe . . ."

"Look, our marriage isn't *all* about sex. Now come to bed so we can make mad, passionate love."

I look at him. "Right, and ruin a perfectly good brownie?"

Twenty-five

I'D RATHER EAT
CHOCOLATE

*M*y journey through sex and marriage has left both me and Kip knowing that I am a woman, and that unless Kip turns gay, he's unlikely to find a partner as eager for sex as he is. Probably the most profound thing I've learned from my experiences and my research is that there is a very significant biological difference in the sex drives of men and women, and in my view, this natural limit to our sexual appetites should be acknowledged and respected. And if men can't understand, accept, or sympathize with that, maybe it's time for us to make some noise about it. I am for more open, brutally honest communication about the male sex drive and what it means in a monogamous relationship. Sometimes it hurts. I've lied, he's lied. If anything, my lie, in the very beginning, before we were married, was worse—it wasn't even a lie of omission. When confronted, I said straight out that I wanted a full sexual relationship with Kip. I kept lying and faking until we were already very emotionally involved. I didn't want to lose him.

But I can't react out of fear or guilt anymore. That's over. Now we have a pretty good understanding of each other. I know I have to be prepared to walk away from my marriage if Kip should be unable to respect me, as much as he has the right to walk away. It's a two-way street. It's not always about understanding male sexuality, it's also about seeing women's sexuality outside the context of male happiness. And I think Kip and I are making genuine progress in that direction.

Polly Young-Eisendrath, like some of the other sexperts I've read, believes that since women routinely put men's sexual pleasure before their own (I guess like giving head instead of getting it), women don't know the pleasure sex can hold for them. In other words, they don't know what they're missing. And because they don't know how to find the joys of sex, sex may *seem* quite the unpalatable activity. Thus, appropriately, Young-Eisendrath uses the taste of a "wonderful, exotic [but yucky-looking] Colombian yam" as a metaphor.

She says that when confronted with a dessert menu and the choice of this exotic yam over a well-loved dessert, women would probably choose their favorite dessert. In any case, we wouldn't salivate over the yam until we had tasted it, and liked it. Her opinion is that if you haven't tasted the pleasure, then you won't feel the desire. Thus many more women than men lack sexual desire because the female sexual experience has not been reliably pleasurable.

I'm assuming Young-Eisendrath chose the example of a yam because it may look ugly and unappetizing on the outside, especially on a dessert cart next to the éclairs and chocolate tortes. But perhaps this frog of a dessert will turn into a royally delicious experience once you lick it. Yes, we're talking about sex. It may seem unappetizing, but once you truly taste how delicious it can be, you'll want it again and again and again.

I am curious what those other desserts on the menu are supposed to represent. Perhaps all those things I would choose to do rather than have sex? Maybe they represent reading, relaxing in front of a rerun of *Seinfeld,* snuggling, or eating an éclair. Is sex usually better than going to the mall for lunch and a half-price sale at Macy's?

If all of the above were on a dessert cart with that Colombian yam, and I had my druthers, I would pick the yam way last. What's funny is that women aren't even picking the yam last because it's next to their favorite desserts. The yam's only competition may be a plateful of yucky chores. The yam often loses out to washing the dishes, washing the clothes, vacuuming the carpet, and figuring out the tax returns. I'm sorry. I've tried boiling it, frying it, baking and battering it. I've rented videos and watched others prepare and enjoy their yams. I've tried focusing intently on the sensation of eating the yam so that I might enjoy it without being self-conscious about how I looked while eating it. I've tried to remember that yams are healthy for us. I've bought book after book of yam recipes. I've watched television shows instructing us on the latest techniques of enjoying yams. There are suction devices to increase the blood flow to the tongue so that we may enjoy its flavor more. I've tried yams with marshmallows, with brown sugar, with cinnamon—and still, I do not crave the yam.

Men don't need to go through all this. They don't only love and enjoy sex, which they do, but they also feel an urgent, eager, unambiguous physical desire for sexual release. Any kind. Whether pornographic fantasy or a hastily done blow job from anyone resembling a female in the back of a cab (Hugh Grant).

Women are so very different from that. After all the effort on our behalf and all the breakthroughs ballyhooed, women still must be prodded into sex. We are told just how appetizing and great-tasting it is if only: *if only we gave it a chance, if only our partner beamed in on our clit, if only we escaped cultural brainwashing or our own inhibitions.* If women constantly need to be baited into sex, it's because they don't find sex *that* exciting, period. I doubt that women will ever become so enthralled by sex that they become like men, seeking it everywhere, fervently looking for a chance to get some. Unlike men, who experience sex as a pressing physical need, sex will remain for women a weaker, more fleeting desire. You *can* make the sex act more pleasurable for women, but I don't think we'll ever get to the point where the mere thought of lots of kinky sex will fill us with joy.

Given the choice between the yam (sex) and the chocolate (chocolate), I'd still rather eat chocolate.

Acknowledgments

One of the best parts of writing this book is doing the acknowledgments. By the time you're writing the acknowledgments, the book is written, the last draft accepted, and the second third of your advance check (so sorely needed) is rolling in.

So now I write this with an exhale of relief. This is my time to look back to the very beginning when someone in New York opened a two-page letter and liked the idea within it. That someone was Jessica Papin of Dystel & Goderich Literary Agency. And when Jessica moved on to other ventures, Jane Dystel stepped in and took me under her wing. I cannot imagine a more responsive, 24/7, Johnny-on-the-spot agent. The woman never sleeps. She's tough as nails when looking out for her clients' interests while still being an approachable source of knowledge and support. Whether it's one of her celebrity authors or a fledgling writer, Jane makes you feel equal in priority and importance. Jane Dystel, and her agency, deserve their renown. Jane, thanks for having my back.

To my editor, Kris Puopolo, at Broadway Books: When you write a memoir, there is often the tendency to bleed too much onto the page. My first draft did this in a voluminous flood of thoughts and feelings. My many thanks for your clear eye in helping me rein the book back in, making for a more succinct, to the point, and thus a far more relatable-to and enjoyable read. Even though she had loads of books on the line, she never let on, making me feel like I was the only author she had. And Kris is a perfectionist. In her case, I don't think it's a Freudian character flaw, but one she purposely developed out of respect for her writers and the books they produce. As frustrating as the editorial process can be, Kris was always willing to read the manuscript over and over and over, sometimes late into the night and again in the early morning hours. Even in last-minute time crunches, Kris never let exhaustion get in the way of her unparalleled attention to detail. Thank you for pushing this book to be the best it could be. You can be sure that any success this book enjoys is a result of its been blessed by both your editorial and promotional talents.

Brianne Ramagosa, come on out and take your bow. Brianne is Kris's editorial assistant. She's an angel who goes the extra mile. And she knows how to deftly handle author breakdowns.

Here's to all the folks at Broadway Books who are my unsung heroes. From the folks in publicity that brainstorm ways to get this book heard, to the bleary-eyed but scrupulous copyeditors, proofreaders, and production people who keep it from embarrassing errors and give it a smart look.

And here's to the brothers Bob and Joey Stanley who gave me

some unvarnished truths about male sexuality when this book was only a twinkle in my eye. To Lena B.—we've been going in and out of each other's life for years and years like a needlepoint stitch. Sarah H.—you'll make it into the next book. Final cuts are tough.

Finally, to my sweet husband, Kip. Boy, did you go through the wringer. We lived what I wrote. At times it felt like a reality show with my pen as camera. Though you weren't too keen on exposing your personal life, you have been so supportive. Kip shored me up when my own resolve failed. I know how really tough it was to do that because as exciting as it was to write about our lives, it was also very emotional. This book put us both on a roller coaster of introspection that could be both thrilling and yet nauseating too. Thank God we have a sense of humor. And chocolate. And I want to thank you, Kip, for being my pre-editor editor. Many times I'd sit at the computer, loads of pages strewn all over the floor, pulling out my hair wondering what the sense of it all was. And just as quick as I was to say, "This is all garbage!" Kip was just as quick to pick up the pages, look them over carefully, and say, "No, it's salvageable." He'd read through those pages and tell me where I got all scrambled up. Like a magician with a deck of cards, he'd shuffle the pages into an order that made sense. If it weren't for him, this book would've stopped at the wastepaper basket. Thank you, I love you.

Notes

CHAPTER ONE

4   "We have sex about every . . .": *The Oprah Winfrey Show*, June 27, 2000.

5   "How often do you have . . .": *Berman & Berman: For Women Only*, "Sex: What's Normal?," aired November 25, 2002." Transcripts of show posted on newshe.com.

CHAPTER TWO

9   "Any man or woman . . .": *Not Tonight Dear*, Anthony Pietropinto, M.D., and Jacqueline Simenauer (New York: Doubleday, 1990), 94.

9   "Any efforts to quantify . . .": Kathleen Deveny, "We're Not in the Mood," *Newsweek*, June 30, 2003.

10   For example, Love talks about one of . . .: Patricia Love and Jo Robinson, *Hot Monogamy* (New York: Plume, 1995), 70.

CHAPTER SIX

31   "Women need to be turned . . .": Barbara DeAngelis, *What Women
      Want Men to Know* (New York: Hyperion, 2001), 315.

32   "need to be relaxed . . .": ibid.

32   "A lot of men don't realize . . .": *The Oprah Winfrey Show,* February
      14, 2001.

33   "Often it's how you've been treating your . . .": DeAngelis, 319.

33   "to decide if the information . . ." DeAngelis, 316.

CHAPTER SEVEN

38   "As Sean gradually toned down his temper . . ." *The Ladies' Home
      Journal*, November 2002.

CHAPTER EIGHT

46   "Many times a woman is potentially . . .": John Gray, *Mars and Venus
      in the Bedroom* (New York: HarperCollins, 1995), 89.

47   "Is there a part of you that wants . . .": ibid., 89–90.

48   "By making quickies guilt free . . .": ibid., 82–83.

50   "Although most men . . .": ibid., 77.

52   "The value of sex . . .": Pamela Lister and Redbook, *Married Lust*
      (New York: Hearst Books, 2001), 30.

52   "You don't have to worry about pleasuring . . .": ibid., 143.

CHAPTER NINE

55   "But what if you don't feel. . . .": Pamela Lister and Redbook, *Married
      Lust* (New York: Hearst Books, 2001), 30.

57   "Personally, I had to hand it to her . . .": ibid., 31.

CHAPTER TEN

61 If women are having . . . : Marcia and Lisa Douglass, *Are We Having Fun Yet?: The Intelligent Woman's Guide to Sex* (New York: Hyperion, 1997), 15.

63 "To be honest, I think . . .": Patricia Love and Jo Robinson, *Hot Monogamy* (New York: Plume, 1995), 70.

64 "For the first fifteen or twenty . . .": ibid., 68.

CHAPTER TWELVE

74 "getting a chewing out . . .": *O* magazine, "A Lingerie Revolution," July 2003.

75 "A lot of women want to feel . . .": ibid.

76 "Thongs, corsets . . .": ibid.

CHAPTER FIFTEEN

95 "When sex takes on . . .": *O* magazine, July/August 2000.

99 "Our sexuality isn't separate . . .": ibid.

CHAPTER SIXTEEN

100 "the most enjoyable, comfortable . . .": *The Better Sex Video Series.* "Volume 1: Better Sexual Techniques." Sinclair Intimacy Institute.

103 According to Dr. Love, the men say . . . : Patricia Love and Jo Robinson, *Hot Monogamy* (New York: Plume, 1995), 82–83.

103 "What touched Karen most . . .": ibid., 83.

104 "psyche grows harder and smaller . . .": ibid., 83.

104 "A man's persistent sexual . . .": John Gray, *Mars and Venus in the Bedroom* (New York: HarperCollins, 1995), 29.

106 "The husband enjoys the same dream . . .": Simone de Beauvoir, *The Second Sex* (New York: Vintage, 1989) 446.

106 "If you try to divest the thing . . .": Richard Taylor, *Good and Evil* (London: Collier-Macmillan, 1970), 297.

107   "It's clean, it's wholesome . . .": *Dr. Phil*, April 2, 2003.

107   "I am a female in . . .": syndicated columnist Dan Savage, "The Cleveland Scene," February 7–13, 2002.

108   "sexy, degrading, erotic . . .": ibid.

108   "Clearly, it is no form of love . . .": Taylor, 297.

109   "Although society's view of sexuality . . .": Love and Robinson, 69.

110   "Celebrate your mental desire . . .": ibid., 87.

112   "In this particular group . . .": ibid., 82.

CHAPTER SEVENTEEN

114   "Even in these days . . .": Patricia Love and Jo Robinson, *Hot Monogamy* (New York: Plume, 1995), 69.

115   "I felt [the effects of the testosterone injections] within . . .": *Female Misbehavior,* "Max, with Max W. Valerio," a film by Monika Treut (New York: First Run Features, 1993), video recording.

116   Anita apparently concurred . . . : See Max Wolf Valerio, *The Testosterone Files* (Emeryville, CA: Seal Press, 2006).

CHAPTER TWENTY

140   "Okay, what's going on south . . .": Much of this dialogue is compiled from several episodes of *Sex and the City.*

141   "Men Like Blow Jobs . . .": Myreah Moore, *Date Like a Man* (New York: HarperCollins, 2000).

142   "Truly amazing erotic action . . .": Liszt's book is being quoted in *Cosmopolitan*, November 2001.

143   "I have agreed to all . . .": Pamela Lister and Redbook, *Married Lust* (New York: Hearst Books, 2001), 80.

143   "One of the reasons therapists . . .": ibid., 79.

143   "Even if you hate it . . .": ibid., 79.

144   "At some point . . .": ibid., 81.

145   "raunch culture": Ariel Levy, *Female Chauvinist Pigs: Women and the Rise of Raunch Culture* (New York: Free Press, 2006), 80.

146 "At first, they shimmied onstage . . .": ibid., 73.

146 "Despite what can fairly be called . . .": ibid., 81–82.

148 "Giving head can be fun . . .": Moore, 166–67.

149 "As a wife I still know my place . . .": Mo'nique, *The Queens of Comedy* DVD (Paramount 2001).

CHAPTER TWENTY-TWO

171 "It may be a quickie . . .": Pamela Lister and Redbook, *Married Lust*, (New York: Hearst Books, 2001), 143.

CHAPTER TWENTY-FIVE

201 Polly Young-Eisendrath, like some of the other. . . : Polly Young-Eisendrath, *Women and Desire: Beyond Wanting to be Wanted* (New York: Harmony Books, 1999), 60.

ABOUT THE AUTHOR

Joan Sewell has a master's degree in philosophy. She lives in Seattle, Washington, with her husband, Kip. *I'd Rather Eat Chocolate* is her first book.